A Stay-at-Home Mom's Complete Guide to Playgroups

A Stay-at-Home Mom's Complete Guide to Playgroups

Carren W. Joye

Writers Club Press
San Jose New York Lincoln Shanghai

A Stay-at-Home Mom's Complete Guide to Playgroups

Writers Club Press
an imprint of iUniverse.com, Inc.

For information address:
iUniverse.com, Inc.
5220 S 16th, Ste. 200
Lincoln, NE 68512
www.iuniverse.com

Cover art designed by Michael Coley.

ISBN: 0-595-14684-8

Printed in the United States of America

Dedication

This book is dedicated to my husband, Tim, and to my children, Megan, Ashley, Zachary and Windsor, who make being a stay-at-home mom more fun than anything in the world!

Contents

List of Illustrations

A Stay-at-Home Mom's Complete Guide to Playgroups

13.Both adults and children enjoy a birthday party during playgroup...84

14.One mom reads her child's favorite book during playgroup. 88

15.After making their own Easter baskets, the playgroup children gather
   for an Easter Egg Hunt at the park. 93

16.Children enjoy playing in the pool during the summer. 98

17.One little girl plays "Pin the Mouth on the Pumpkin" during a
   Halloween playgroup. 103

18.Playgroup can meet in various locations, such as the local park...115

19.Children enjoy snacks on the deck during playgroup. 120

20.Two playgroups get together for a big party during the summer. 130

21.Children of all ages enjoy examining a helicopter during a home-
   school field trip. 139

22.The boys dig in the sand with one of the dads. 145

Acknowledgements

Books don't write themselves! Although this one has been a nearly effortless and entirely enjoyable project, it did take more than an author to put it all together. It would never have been completed without the help and encouragement of many people along the way, and it would be very thoughtless of me if I did not thank them.

First, I thank my family for all of their support and understanding when I spent so much time on the computer working on the book. Beyond even that, if it weren't for my husband, the Millbrook Area Playgroup would have never been started in the first place and this book would have never been written!

Second, thank you, Mom, for being such an inspirational role model and for talking me through some of the decisions.

Third, thank you, Teresa, for insisting that we keep the playgroup going even when it was reduced to just the two of us! I hope that everyone who participates in a playgroup will find a friend like you.

Finally, I want to thank all the members of the Millbrook Area Playgroup and the other playgroup "veterans" worldwide who submitted suggestions for the playgroup tips on our web site. Those tips have served as the inspiration and foundation for this book.

Introduction

Recently quit working to stay home with your children? Just moved to a new neighborhood? Obviously you have made some important decisions and major changes in your life, but now that you have made them, you may be finding yourself wondering what to do next. As a matter of fact, it's not unlikely that you may be feeling isolated and cut off from the world as a stay-at-home mom in a new neighborhood. Of course, you have your child with you, but you still feel alone. You may even be a bit concerned that your child is lonely as well. These feelings and concerns are normal, so don't start doubting your judgments; instead, take steps to improve matters. Reach out for the support you and your child need.

In 1995, I was in the same position as you are, and my solution was one that I am suggesting to you now: Start a playgroup! Right now, you can benefit from something I didn't have at that time; that is, a book that will take you step by step through the process of starting and maintaining a playgroup written by a stay-at-home mom who has founded of five successful playgroups.

Why This Book?

My efforts since 1995 have produced not only five active playgroups, but also lifelong friends for my four children and me. In addition, I have been able to share my playgroup experiences with literally hundreds of at-home moms and their playgroups all around the world via the Internet, first with MillbrookPlaygroup.com and then with

OnlinePlaygroup.com. Ever since the web site for our playgroup was first designed in 1998, fellow stay-at-home moms from all over the United States and from as far away as Japan and Switzerland have addressed two questions over and over again: How did your playgroup get started? And, how can I start a playgroup?

In researching materials to answer the latter question, I found very little resources beyond a short chapter here and there in various books for at-home moms and a few articles in women's magazines highlighting the basics of starting a playgroup. Gathering information from my own experiences as well as from the experiences of other playgroup "veterans," I collected tips for starting a playgroup for a page on our web site. As the tips increased, I realized many of them could be expanded to include step-by-step instructions for starting and maintaining a playgroup.

At the same time, I began to receive email from moms and dads thanking our playgroup for providing information that was sorely lacking and gravely needed and asking for even more practical help in starting their own playgroups. I was delighted to offer advice and share my experiences with them as I helped them start their playgroups and keep their playgroups going.

When I co-founded a local homeschool support group for parents and their children, I applied the playgroup tips to organizing it and realized these "playgroup tips" would assist any number of groups, not just preschool playgroups. Again, a little market research revealed an untapped niche market. Perhaps other stay-at-home moms and homeschooling families would benefit from a book that takes them step-by-step to starting and maintaining their own playgroups, custom designed to fit their needs as well as those of their children. *A Stay-At-Home Mom's Complete Guide to Playgroups* was born.

Finally, a book that can answer any question regarding how to start a playgroup, any kind of playgroup, and how to keep one going! Sure, many national mothers' organizations feature playgroups as a benefit to their members, and some moms may prefer joining these established groups. Indeed, these organizations boast thousands of members. However, some areas of the country do not have local chapters of the national organizations, nor do all local chapters feature playgroups as a benefit. *A Stay-At-Home Mom's Complete Guide to Playgroups* maintains that you can start your own playgroup without the assistance of a national organization, if there's not one available. Besides, what works in one part of the country does not always work in another, and what one group wants may not appeal to another group of moms. In addition, anyone can start a playgroup with little or no initial expenditure of money and with minimal investment of her valuable and limited time. She can custom design the perfect playgroup for herself and her child and find other moms who want the same thing.

It's easy, once you know how! And this book will show you how by taking you through each step and giving you options along the way. As a result, not only will your playgroup be custom-designed for you and your child, but it will also be a successful playgroup for as long as you need it.

How Our Playgroup Started

I didn't know I was custom designing a playgroup in early 1995 when I first began thinking about the need for a playgroup in my hometown. Then, as now, our relatives lived two states away, so we didn't have that essential support system of an extended family. At that time, my little family of four had been living in our new home for less than three months. I loved our bigger home, although the neighborhood didn't have any young children or stay-at-home moms. I had resigned my position in public relations at a local university the year before to stay home and raise our children. I loved being a stay-at-home mom, although I sometimes felt isolated at home with a preschooler and a toddler. I didn't regret my decision to quit working, but I did miss the camaraderie of my colleagues, the stimulation of adult conversation, and the busy and active lifestyle I used to lead. I also missed the friends we had left in our old neighborhood, and I wasn't the only one who did.

"Mommy, when am I going to play with my friends?" my four-year-old daughter, Megan, asked me. Sharing her playtime exclusively with her baby sister was becoming boring. She sincerely missed her little friends.

What could I do? Fighting city traffic on the way to our old neighborhood to meet our old friends on any regular basis was out of the question. Once or twice, maybe, but that would get old real quick! Unfortunately, our new neighborhood did not have at-home parents or young children.

My husband came up with the solution by accident one evening while dropping off paperwork at a colleague's home in a neighborhood about a mile away. He had literally found a treasury of children in that neighborhood! Toys littered nearly all the yards, and minivans filled the driveways.

"Start your playgroup there," he advised.

I tried not to get too excited as I thought about weekly playgroup sessions and impromptu afternoon playdates, someone to talk to about parenting issues and something to do besides sing nursery rhymes and change diapers!

I didn't know how to begin and there were no books to serve as resources, so I just jumped in! We drove through the neighborhood writing down the addresses of every single house on every street. I wrote a letter addressed to "Neighbor" explaining that I was a stay-at-home mom with preschool children seeking others to start a playgroup. We mailed 92 letters, and I waited anxiously for responses. *What if no one responded? What if I got 30 calls?* I didn't know what to expect, and I didn't have a plan for either scenario. I just hoped and prayed for the best.

Fortunately, eight stay-at-home moms called within the next two weeks. Perfect! I scheduled our first meeting for the following Wednesday morning at my house.

Next dilemma! How do I prepare? I had some idea of what to expect because I had started a playgroup in our old neighborhood about eight months before we moved. I planned to adopt what worked from that group and to try to avert what didn't work. However, like the old saying that every pregnancy is different, so I learned quickly that every playgroup is different as well. Some ideas worked; others had to be changed a bit; while still others were completely unsuited to this particular group of moms.

Since then, the Millbrook Area Playgroup has gone through a number of transformations, and the members have made a few adjustments here and there to make it better for both the moms and our children. Best of all, not only have the moms made some lifelong friends among our group, but our children have as well. Indeed, all of my four children have made their first friends at playgroup, even baby Windsor.

Only I remain from the original nine moms, but I still keep in touch with the other eight, as well as with more than fifty other moms and dads who have been playgroup participants at one time or another over these last years. They are now scattered all over the U.S. and the world, from Florida to California to Guam! And they are all repeatedly amazed and pleased to hear that our playgroup is still going strong.

Actually, many former participants have enjoyed our playgroup so much that they have started their own playgroups in their new hometowns, using MillbrookPlaygroup.com and OnlinePlaygroup.com as valuable practical resources. With this book, our playgroup can reach even more at-home parents, both moms and dads, who seek peers for themselves and their children in a career field that can be isolating, sometimes confusing and often contradictory, yet always deeply satisfying. As in any career field, to be truly happy as a stay-at-home parent, you need support, encouragement and advice from veterans in the field. For colleagues like that, you need a playgroup.

What Is a Playgroup Exactly?

For a stay-at-home parent, playgroup is quality time with your peers—yours and your child's! Where else can you find support, encouragement, advice—in short, friendship? So if you don't have a playgroup, find one or start one!

A playgroup is any gathering of children, generally with their primary caregivers, on a regular basis. Playgroups are wonderful opportunities for children to play together and for their parents to socialize. Indeed, playgroups are as important for the moms as they are for the children. Stay-at-home parents need the support and encouragement that a playgroup provides just as their toddlers and preschoolers need the socialization.

Playgroups give moms a chance to make new friends, to share problems with other moms who have older children, or just to get out of the house. Only other stay-at-home moms can understand exactly how isolated you sometimes feel and can provide insight into dealing with the unique problems associated with being at home. After all, who else can give you firsthand advice about dealing with infant sleeping problems, potty training or sibling rivalry? Not only that, but you can see for yourself how others handle certain discipline situations, and decide for yourself what works and what does not.

In today's society many new mothers not only have postponed having children, but also have moved great distances from their families and friends. They no longer have that built-in support system that all new moms need. Playgroups fill that gap.

Generally composed of stay-at-home moms who realize a need for social interaction for their children, playgroups give children a chance to play with others besides their own siblings. Playgroups can be the ideal introduction to socialization for the preschool set. Whether an informal hour of free play or a more structured period with a story time or craft, playgroups can be tailored to any group of children. While the children play together, they gain valuable social skills for school, learning how to share and take turns. In a playgroup setting, they often form their first lasting friendships.

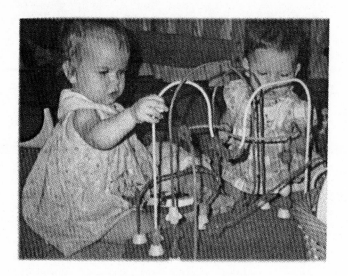

What to Expect from This Book

Whether you are seeking support for yourself or little friends for your child, you will find what you need to start and maintain your own successful, custom-designed playgroup from the information in this book. Unlike other books for at-home moms that may devote one chapter to starting playgroups, *A Stay-At-Home Mom's Complete Guide to Playgroups* provides helpful instructions and practical suggestions for starting and maintaining different kinds of playgroups and mothers' groups without bogging down in minute and needless details. Additionally, this book covers ways in which the Internet can help. In this digital age, the Internet can only help any organization, and every chapter contains some reference to the Internet at every stage of creating your playgroup. One entire chapter is devoted to how you can use the Internet for promotion, information and organization of your playgroup.

However, while the Internet is a valuable resource, let me stress that you do not need to be online to have a successful playgroup.

Although *A Stay-At-Home Mom's Complete Guide to Playgroups* features a week-by-week guide of children's activities, the activities are purposely limited to 52 simple crafts and games that a playgroup can use to get started for one year. The object of the book is to get the playgroup started, not to list craft ideas.

This guidebook will not only help you get your playgroup started, it will also help you maintain it successfully. Use this book to assist you with:

- Planning what kind of playgroup would best serve your needs.
- Finding other moms and children who want the same thing.
- Using the Internet to help your playgroup.
- Setting guidelines and establishing rules.
- Preparing to host a group in your home.
- Providing extra services and benefits.
- Planning special activities.
- Functioning as the leader of a successful playgroup.
- Troubleshooting any potential problems.
- Creating special playgroups for homeschooling families, at-home dads, working parents, adopted children, premature babies, children with disabilities, and more!

All to help you and the other moms and children enjoy the benefits of a successful playgroup!

A note here about the term "moms" in reference to playgroups: "Moms" mean at-home moms, working moms, work-at-home moms, single parents, homeschooling parents or even at-home dads! Playgroups are not exclusive to stay-at-home moms, so don't let that prevent you from starting your own playgroup, however you conceive a playgroup to be. Also, don't delay starting a playgroup just because you think your child is too young. You'll be surprised how much you'll both get out of it!

And now, here's one early piece of advice in getting your playgroup off the ground, and it's really a simple two-parter: Decide to do it, and then do it!

CHAPTER 1

DESIGNING A PLAYGROUP FOR YOU AND YOUR CHILD

Take a few minutes to think about what you want in a playgroup. What would be the perfect group for you and your child? To find out, you need to ask yourself a few fundamental questions. Just preschoolers, or infants and toddlers too? Just a social playtime, or structured activities? Will the group meet year-round, or only during the school year? Some of these questions will be answered automatically without giving them much thought—you know what you and your child need—but others may require you to think about what you really want out of a playgroup and how much time you want to devote to managing it.

Basically, this chapter will help you custom design your playgroup. Through a series of questions, you will:

- Decide if you want a children's playgroup, a mothers' group, or a combination.
- Determine the desired age-range for children.
- Consider the preferable number of participants.
- Decide what you want to do with your group.

- Choose a day and time most convenient for you.
- Select a location.

After you have made some initial choices and decisions, you can find other moms who want the same thing. The other parents involved in the playgroup should be as interested as you are in it and have similar goals for the group, so during the first gathering of your playgroup, discuss these issues and the preliminary decisions you have made. You may need to modify the original goals slightly to accommodate their requirements. As the months go by, your playgroup is likely to develop and change to accommodate the changing needs of parents and children, but these questions will get you started in the right direction.

Who is the group for?

This question is most important because many of the other decisions will be based upon how you answer this one. Will this be a mothers' group, where the moms meet for crafts or seminars about motherhood issues during a special time without interruptions from the children? Or will this be strictly a playgroup, centered on children, where the moms and children interact together with structured mom-child play?

There are several issues to consider. An organization devoted to moms requires child supervision; would the moms rotate or will you collectively hire a babysitter? A babysitter would allow everyone the chance to participate in the group sessions without having to miss one in order to watch the children. A nominal fee should cover the expenses of babysitters as well as the costs of craft supplies and the fees of special lecturers. A mothers' group will be more likely to handle a large number of members successfully without risk of there being too many. Although a large group loses the intimacy of a smaller gathering, it has the advantage of additional benefits and services for its members, such as newsletters, playgroups divided by age, family functions, and possible discounts at local stores.

Most likely a mothers' group will need to meet in a central location where the children can be cared for in a separate, but nearby room. Churches and community centers are ideal locations. Try to find one that will let you meet without charge, otherwise your membership dues will have to cover the rental of the facilities.

On the other hand, if your group is centered on the children, you can meet in each other's homes where toys will be plentiful. Membership dues would not be necessary since you will not have to rent space, buy craft supplies or hire babysitters. The only cost involved would be the cost of snacks when it is your turn to host playgroup. Groups centered on the children tend to be smaller, simply because of limited space in homes. Groups of ten moms or less can meet comfortably in each other's homes.

The interaction between moms in a playgroup of this type tends to facilitate friendships more quickly, mainly because your attention is not directed to making a craft or listening to a speaker. Your children are right there among you all. You have an opportunity to ask advice, share experiences and see firsthand how other mothers handle discipline situations. In addition, neighborhood playgroups are generally more informal and spontaneous than larger and more structured groups.

You may opt for a more exclusive playgroup with benefits for both parents and children. You can form a playgroup for:

- Families with an only child
- Boys only or girls only
- Adopted children
- Premature babies
- Children with special needs
- First-time parents
- Single parents
- Younger moms or older moms
- Working moms or at-home moms
- At-home dads

- Homeschooling families
- Specific ethnic or religious groups

You can design your playgroup any way you want! Once you have decided what kind of playgroup you want, you can target potential members more effectively.

What ages do you want the children to be?

If you have decided to create a playgroup centered on the children, what ages do you want them to be? Naturally, somewhere around your own children's ages! But think for a moment. What about older or younger siblings of the other children who may be in the playgroup? Will they be invited? Also, your baby may be only six months old now, but should you limit the ages of the children to six to twelve months? After all, eventually even your baby will be too old for the group!

On the other hand, you could start with a playgroup designed for an exclusive age range just to establish the members. Then, as all the children grow, the age range of the playgroup expands and changes to reflect the new ages. Many playgroups begin this way, and the children grow up together and eventually start school in the same classes together.

Indeed, the ideal playgroup will have children who are close in age. Since babies and toddlers are at different stages of development, grouping them together can sometimes be difficult, especially if the children are involved in structured activities. However, age differences sometimes work very well. Younger children like to emulate the play of older kids, and babies usually enjoy watching older children play.

Use your judgment when organizing your playgroup, keeping in mind the number of children, size of the meeting space, and the area in which you live. Some areas of the country have fewer stay-at-home moms because of a higher cost of living, for example. As a result, you may find it difficult to find enough stay-at-home moms with children who are in the same age range. Simply finding any children at home at all may force you to admit older or younger children than you originally intended!

What is the ideal size for a playgroup?

The ideal size for a playgroup varies depending on the purpose of the playgroup, the location, and the needs of your child. You can have a playgroup with only two moms and two children, if a playgroup is what you want to call it. That was the case with the Millbrook Area Playgroup at one time. After the first year or so, most of the original moms had moved or their children had started school, so the playgroup dwindled down to only three moms and four children. Then one of those moms moved away. The remaining mom and I continued to meet every Wednesday morning for "playgroup"—never mind the fact that all of us spent time together nearly every day already! The point is that we needed to have a special time set aside each week above and beyond the other activities we shared together. That spring, when we distributed flyers around town, our playgroup grew to 11 moms and 19 children, and we were so happy that we had not ended playgroup just because we'd had only two members!

Most playgroups designed for the socialization of the children remain purposely small and intimate, with less than ten moms. Fewer members mean fewer children, so they are easier to supervise, and they get to know each other more quickly.

When the playgroups are held in homes, the hostess prefers a small group too! In that case, about eight to ten members are an ideal number. That way, the members have to host playgroup only about every eight to ten weeks, and the group won't be too large even if everyone participates that week. Not every member will be able to attend playgroup every week, so even with several sick or vacationing members, the playgroup should still have an adequate and enjoyable number of participants that week. In comparison, with a very small group of only three or four, the members are likely to dislike having to host so frequently, and playgroup may actually have to be cancelled a number of times because of a couple of sick or vacationing members.

Mothers' groups, on the other hand, usually include many members because they meet in a central location with a separate group for moms and sometimes two or three separate groups of children, depending on their ages. The larger the group is, the more revenue from membership dues there will be, and therefore, the more benefits and services the group can provide. As a result, it is to the advantage of a mothers' group to be fairly large.

Whether to make your playgroup large or small may depend largely on what works best for your child. Consider his personality. Is he outgoing and quick to join a group or does he need time to feel comfortable in new surroundings? Does he thrive in stimulating environments? Or do noise and activity overwhelm him? Is he an active child or is he more quiet and observant? Your child's personality will help you choose the best playgroup environment for him.

Keep in mind that more children mean more noise and activity. Most children fare better in small groups of six to ten, but the younger the children, the smaller the group should be. Again, it is important to consider your own child's personality.

Just a social playtime or structured activities?

There are advantages and disadvantages to both. If the children are close in age, some sort of structured activities may work very well. Simple crafts geared for their age, songs and dances, finger plays, story time, and games will facilitate learning and socialization. In addition, activities involving both mother and child can create a special time together.

However, what about the parent who has twins or two children only nine months apart? She will have to divide her time between the two, and that may not be as relaxing as a playgroup could be. In addition, if all of the children in playgroup represent a broad range of ages, such group activities would prove unfeasible. What would appeal to one group would be too babyish for another.

If playgroup is strictly a social playtime, the children can play while the moms talk. The moms get to know each other better, form friendships, seek advice and share experiences. The playgroup environment then becomes a support group for the parents as well as a social playtime for the children. If the playgroup includes a wide range of ages, this type of playgroup works best. A social playtime gives the children a chance to explore and experiment without having them work on any particular skill other than socialization. After all, play is children's work.

Additionally, you need to consider the size of the group and the level of stimulation with which your child is comfortable. Does your child thrive in stimulating environments? Or do noise and activity overwhelm him? Is he an active child or is he more quiet and observant? Let your child's personality determine the most appropriate activities, whether they are structured activities, free playtime, or a combination of both.

What kinds of structured activities?

If you decide you want to offer activities for the group, you should plan for children who are about the same age and select activities that are age-appropriate. Read the chapter "Week-by-Week Guide of Children's Activities" for 52 various crafts, games, songs and activities that appeal to children ages 20 months to five years old. For other ideas, check out the books in your local library or bookstore. Also, go to TheIdeaBox.com, ParentSoup.com or FamilyFun.com for excellent suggestions.

Keep in mind that the average child's attention span on any one activity is about ten to fifteen minutes! As a result, it may be a good idea to start playgroup with a structured activity and end with free playtime.

Also, keep in mind that the playgroup is not meant to be a preschool, so keep it relaxed and informal.

If you decide on activities, you also need to decide how the craft supplies will be provided. Each parent can bring supplies for her child, or the hostess each week can provide the materials, or membership dues can cover the supplies.

Should snacks be served during playgroup?

Snacks are a great way to break the ice, especially during the first meeting of a new group. Also, snack time can effectively divide the time between free play and structured activities if your playgroup engages in both. Generally, serve snacks about a half-hour after playgroup has begun or shortly after everyone has arrived.

The time of day the group meets will determine the type of snacks, if any. A group that meets early in the morning may prefer breakfast items, such as muffins and juice. On the other hand, a group that meets close to noon may opt for no snacks at all or may want to share lunch together. The hostess could provide the entrée and the others could bring assigned side dishes, desserts and beverages.

Generally, however, most playgroups prefer a light snack, provided by the hostess. Snacks do not have to be elaborate or costly; combinations of fruit, cookies, chips and dip with soft drinks, milk and juice should suffice. At the very least, drinks should be offered. On the other hand, some moms use the playgroup as an opportunity to indulge their love of cooking, and they prepare all sorts of delicious treats for their playgroup guests. The Millbrook Area Playgroup had one member who could duplicate the appetizers at our favorite restaurants, and we all looked forward to playgroup at her house!

Keep in mind that some parents do not allow their children to eat sweets between meals. During the first meeting, you may want to offer a variety of refreshments, ranging from healthy snacks such as fruits and bran muffins to sweets such as cookies, so that parents will have a choice for their children. At that time, determine any restrictions or allergies. Repeat this process periodically as new moms and children join the playgroup. Prepare to be tolerant and flexible.

When is the best time to schedule playgroup?

Do you work and/or do you want to include working moms? If so, the playgroup will need to meet in the evenings or on weekends to accommodate work schedules. Keep in mind that younger children tend to get cranky in the evenings, so the morning or early afternoon on Saturday may be best. However, if you save your weekends for family outings, then pick a weekday afternoon to have playgroup.

For primarily stay-at-home moms, weekdays are usually best. Again, mornings are usually better than afternoons because of nap times, but that depends on the age of the children. When selecting a time in the morning, consider what time your children and the other children wake up. Parents of early birds may not mind an early playgroup that starts at 9 a.m., but those with children who sleep late will always arrive late, so you may want to accommodate those families. On the other hand, those children who wake early will be cranky before the others will. Also, consider how long it will take people to drive to the playgroup location before you set a time for playgroup to begin.

If any weekday suits your schedule, you still may want to limit the choices before you ask for input from other moms. Keep in mind that many families may take three-day weekend holidays, so Friday may not be a good day. You may have to cancel playgroup occasionally because of an expected low turnout before a holiday or even during the summer.

For various reasons, Monday is not a good choice either. Families usually gear up for the week on Mondays, or catch up on housework they neglected over the weekend. Besides, it's hard to prepare for guests if you expect them on a Monday.

That leaves Tuesday, Wednesday and Thursday for your playgroup. As you talk with other moms who indicate an interest in joining the group, you can find out if you need to eliminate another day automatically. Some may have children who attend a Mom's Day Out program once or twice a week, so those days would not be favorable.

Finally, if all things seem about equal, pick the day that is most convenient for you. The group can always decide to change it later. However, once the playgroup agrees to a scheduled day and time, the group should stick to it. You may be inclined to want to be as flexible as possible so that everyone will be able to attend, by having each hostess pick the day and time during her week, for example. Unfortunately, a successful playgroup cannot be that flexible. A variable meeting schedule can cause confusion, and the playgroup's momentum will be lost. Your members need to know that playgroup meets on a certain day at a certain time, so they will be able to schedule other activities and appointments around it.

How long should playgroup last?

This depends on the ages of the children. The younger the children are, the less time playgroup needs to be. They simply become too cranky, causing needless conflicts because they are so irritable. Keep playgroup sessions to about an hour and a half for children younger than three years old. Generally, two hours seem to work best with a wide range of ages. Parents with younger children can always leave early if they feel the need.

How frequently should playgroup meet?

Children interact best when they feel comfortable in their surroundings and are with people they know. Repetition breeds familiarity. The more frequently the group meets, the sooner the children will get to know each other and develop friendships. Some playgroups meet twice a week, but a weekly playgroup would just as easily serve your purpose. A weekly routine is easier to schedule around, so moms would be less likely to forget the meeting and accidentally miss it. It becomes a habit and something they can look forward to each week.

However, if you and the other moms are busy with other activities, or if the cost of hosting playgroup prohibits weekly meetings, then a biweekly playgroup may be best. Don't meet any less frequently than that, and definitely have the hostess call everyone in advance as a reminder if the group meets only twice a month. One Seattle mom who attended a biweekly playgroup recalls the time she and her daughter arrived at a neighbor's house for playgroup, only to be met at the door by the distressed hostess just getting out of the shower. She had completely forgotten about playgroup!

Will the playgroup meet year-round or exclusively during the school year?

You will miss your playgroup friends during the summer! And so will your child! For many stay-at-home moms, the summer months are no different than the winter months—they are still home alone with their toddler or preschooler. Also, keep in mind that once an organization breaks for the summer, it can be difficult to resuscitate it again a few months later. Besides, the warmer months mean you can meet in a greater variety of places, like the park or the zoo.

However, some moms in the group may have older children who attend school. Having several older siblings suddenly joining the playgroup and considerably expanding the size of the group will not only be stressful but may also make the group too large to meet comfortably in a home. At the same time, maybe you will be busy with your own older children who are out of school for the summer, by going on vacations to the beach, visiting relatives far away, and enjoying other summertime commitments. In that case, you and your children won't need playgroup for social interaction during the summer.

What about holidays?

Holidays, such as Christmas, Easter or Spring Break, mean siblings out of school who may join playgroup and make the group larger. Depending on how many older children there will be, you may want to take a break from playgroup during holidays. Besides, many families travel out of town or expect relatives to visit over the holidays. Along with holiday shopping and social activities, everyone in playgroup may be stretched to the limit!

Get a consensus on what others want to do. They may want to cancel playgroup for a couple of weeks, or it's possible that two or three families have no plans for traveling, hosting relatives, or entertaining and may welcome a chance to meet for playgroup.

Where is the ideal location for playgroup to meet?

The ideal location depends on the number of members in your playgroup, what your playgroup does, and what their desires are. Some popular locations include:

- Your homes
- Parks or playgrounds
- Facilities such as a church, community center, library, or YMCA
- Fast food restaurants with play areas
- Different area attractions such as the beach, zoo, amusement park, and museum

A small group of about ten or fewer moms may meet comfortably in each other's homes. Indeed, everyone may prefer meeting in the warm, intimate atmosphere of a home rather than an impersonal location like a community center or church. However, consider who will clean up after playgroup. As the hostess in your home, not only will you clean your house before playgroup arrives, but you may also end up doing all the cleaning once everyone leaves, unless a couple of considerate moms linger to help. On the other hand, the entire group must be responsible for tidying up after a session in a community center or church.

If your playgroup engages in structured activities for the children or the parents, a large facility may be more convenient no matter how much more you prefer meeting in each other's homes. The size of the homes matters even if you meet for just a social playtime; for example, military base housing and apartments are generally small and have limited parking. In addition, some families collect antiques or expensive art—two things that don't mix well with children!

However, if one mom's home is inconvenient, she can always "share" playgroup with another mom. In this case, one has playgroup in her home while the other provides the snacks. To ensure that all goes well, the one bringing snacks should consider what the other mom usually serves, make sure she brings enough for everyone who may attend, and stay to help clean up afterwards.

An alternative would be for playgroup to meet at a park or playground, with the hostess providing the snacks or everyone bringing snacks to share. Although a park will accommodate large numbers very well, this location is not conducive to intimacy. It's hard to carry on a conversation with other adults if one or more of you are chasing your preschoolers around. It's also harder for the children to get to know each other in a playground setting because the playground is open to many other children besides the playgroup.

If you must meet in a park, try to arrange some type of crafts for the children during part of the playgroup session. Perhaps begin playgroup with free playtime, followed by snacks, then a structured activity or craft, and end with free playtime. That way, both children and parents will have the opportunity to socialize on a more intimate basis during the snack time and craft.

Another consideration is that parents with more than one child may feel uncomfortable going to the park on a regular basis, especially if the park is not enclosed. It is difficult to keep a close eye on two or more children who are exploring different areas of the park at the same time.

Then, of course, the weather is a prime consideration. Aside from inclement weather, some days will likely be too hot or too cold to enjoy playing outdoors at the park.

The park is not the only option though. Some locations that may be inclined to offer facilities for free or for a minimal fee are churches, community centers, neighborhood clubhouses, hospitals, libraries, and

YMCAs. Ask around. Perhaps one of your playgroup members or their spouses may have an ideal suggestion.

Area attractions may suit your playgroup better. Meet at different locations each week, such as the beach, lake, zoo and mall. Go to amusement parks, water parks, museums, arcades and fast-food restaurants with play areas. Depending on the children's ages, you could also take them bowling, roller skating and swimming. Although playgroups forming in small towns will probably be limited in their choice of area attractions, those in large cities or tourist areas will probably have a variety from which to choose.

In any case, consider all of these suggestions before determining the best location for your playgroup. Even if your group intends to find a large, central location, you can always do what our homeschool group did for the first two meetings and meet for the first time in a home. Indeed, it may be preferable because a home projects a warmth and friendliness you want to convey to the new members of this soon-to-be group of friends.

How much time will it take to manage a playgroup?

Do you want to maintain primary control of the group, or would you feel comfortable delegating some of the responsibilities? That is the real question here. Playgroup will take up as much of your time as you allow it. Generally, however, starting and managing a playgroup in its early stages will take more time than maintaining the playgroup later on, say after about six sessions. In the beginning you will have to do the initial legwork, such as finding other moms who may want to join, setting the groundwork in place for establishing guidelines and rules, scheduling a rotation and finding a central location for meetings. If your group plans special speakers or structured activities for the children, you can expect to spend a little more time organizing these services as well. Also, the larger the group, the more work required to maintain it. Of course, with a larger group, you can also delegate the work. Indeed, you will have to share the workload if your playgroup enjoys very many supplementary activities and services.

You can decide right now to limit your group to a small, intimate number, in which case you may expect to devote your time primarily to keeping up with rotation and perhaps to planning occasional special events. You may need to call or email moms to remind them about the group, be available in case a hostess needs to reschedule at the last minute, and update the playgroup phone list when a new member joins. Periodically, you will need to "recruit" new members by posting or distributing flyers.

Basically, though, playgroup will be fairly low maintenance. For some easy-to-use management tools geared specifically for playgroup maintenance, visit OnlinePlaygroup.com on the Internet.

Just remember though, no matter how large or small your playgroup is, it will not work without someone to keep it going. So, once your playgroup gets off the ground, you will need to attend faithfully and keep the ball rolling.

How much will it cost to participate in a playgroup?

Most neighborhood playgroups are free. The only cost involved is the money that the hostess spends on snacks, and that's something you can control. Playgroups that provide crafts for the children may need a small membership fee to cover expenses, or the hostess could be responsible for the craft supplies each week, or each mom could be responsible for bringing the supplies for her child.

Mothers' groups generally charge nominal membership fees, organize fundraisers, or collect donations to cover such costs as craft supplies, fees for guest speakers, facility rental, and babysitters. Sometimes the money is collected on a session-by-session basis of about $2 to $5 per session. Other groups charge membership dues on a yearly basis, ranging from

$10 to $50, depending on how frequently they meet and how many extra services and benefits they offer.

In your case, before setting membership dues for a large or small group, determine if your group will need the following and consider how much they will cost:

- Facility rental
- Snack supplies
- Craft supplies for children and/or adults
- Fees for guest speakers
- Childcare supervisors
- Special parties or events
- Newsletters or Calendars
- Web site
- Publicity costs, such as printing flyers or posters
- Miscellaneous expenses, such as postage or long distance phone charges

To start a playgroup, the initial costs lie in making copies of the flyers you distribute and paying for postage. Your husband's workplace may have a copy machine that you can use for free; otherwise, check with libraries, copy shops, and local stores for copy machines, and compare prices. They usually charge only a few cents per page, but pennies here and there add up. If you plan to mail playgroup announcements or invitations in area neighborhoods rather than distribute them by hand, you need to consider the cost of postage. In this case, postcards will be more economical than letters or flyers.

Expect to distribute about ten flyers to area businesses and about 50 flyers to individual homes in local neighborhoods. It's up to you exactly how many you need. You could even start off with a small number of flyers, wait for any responses, and do more later if necessary.

How long will it take to get my playgroup off the ground?

The answer to this question depends on a number of factors, one of which is the area of the country in which you live. Some areas have a higher cost of living, and therefore, many more two-income families and fewer stay-at-home moms. The fewer stay-at-home moms there are in your area, the longer it may take to get a playgroup going. Don't get discouraged; simply plan to widen the target area.

Another factor is the method you choose to reach people who may be interested in your playgroup. For example, if all you do is post your intention for a playgroup onto a web site directory, you will certainly get a few responses over time, but probably not enough to start a group. In the two years of having a web site for our playgroup (www.MillbrookPlaygroup.com), only five new members have originated from the Internet. That's not very many considering that the playgroup has had more than 50 total members, with no more than eleven active members at one time. However, Millbrook is a small town; playgroups in larger cities may experience a greater percentage of members originating from the Internet.

Posting flyers in area businesses frequented by at-home moms will generate more responses; this method is often used to "recruit" more moms when the playgroup gets too small. You may want to consider leaving a stack of leaflets in some locations; sometimes people will take leaflets when they won't copy down a phone number from a poster.

However, to reach the greatest number of people interested in joining a playgroup in the shortest amount of time, distribute flyers or mail postcards in neighborhoods with children's toys in the yards. Also, do not discount word-of-mouth. Out of 56 members within the last five years, 25 found out about the Millbrook Area Playgroup from flyers we distributed in their neighborhoods and 21 by word-of-mouth.

With a two-week deadline in which to respond and with at least 50 flyers or postcards to start, depending on how many at-home moms you estimate may live there, you can expect to host your first playgroup within about three weeks. That gives two weeks for them to respond, and one week for you to schedule the day for playgroup and then notify the participants. If your first batch does not generate enough responses after the two-week deadline, mail a second batch. Again, expect to host your first meeting within three weeks of mailing that second batch.

Another factor that may determine how long it takes to start your playgroup is the time of year in which you are trying. Because of family and social commitments, many families are too busy to join a playgroup during the summer months and Christmas holidays. If possible, start your playgroup during the fall when older children have returned to school, late winter when the holidays have ended, or early spring when families are eager to get out of the house. During these seasons, parents are actively seeking activities and social outlets for themselves and their children. As a result, you are more likely to receive quick responses to your first batch of flyers.

During the first couple of playgroup sessions, the group will be getting to know each other and discussing guidelines. After three sessions, your playgroup should be well on the way to being an established organization. However, keep in mind that there may be a time or two when only one mom shows up, particularly in the beginning. This has happened with the Millbrook Area Playgroup a handful of times! Parents are naturally cautious, and they should be. Just don't give up. It may still be a few more sessions before everyone feels like part of a group, but it will happen.

CHAPTER 2

STEP-BY-STEP GUIDE TO STARTING YOUR PLAYGROUP

Starting a neighborhood playgroup is easy and rewarding, and there are many different ways of starting one. Don't delay just because you think your baby may be too young to get anything out of it. You'll be surprised how much a playgroup will do for both of you!

The first step to starting your playgroup is designing what you think will be the perfect group. Just preschoolers, or infants and toddlers too? Just a social playtime, or structured activities? Consider siblings when organizing the playgroup for a certain age range. Also, you need to decide if the group will continue to meet during the summer when there may be several older siblings home during the day, thereby possibly expanding the size of the group considerably. Once you have made preliminary choices and decisions, then you can find others who want the same thing.

Here are nine different ideas for finding or starting a playgroup, with specific step-by-step instructions for the last one. Each idea features both advantages and disadvantages, so you'll know up front what to expect and how to deal with it. Find a method that's right for you—or combine several—and get started!

National Organizations

You can join a local chapter of one of the many national organizations for at-home moms, such as MOMS Club (Moms Offering Moms Support), MOPS (Mothers Of PreSchoolers), and Mothers and More, which used to be FEMALE (Formerly Employed Mothers At the Leading Edge). There are even some national organizations tailored to parents of twins and triplets. Although many national organizations require fees, they are nominal and they cover a variety of services. See the chapter "National Organizations" for an extensive list with contact information.

The main advantage to joining an existing mothers' group is that all the legwork has been done for you. At the same time, however, you may have little or no say in how the group functions because those decisions have already been made. Also, even local chapters tend to have a large number of members. On the one hand, you will find yourself among many likeminded parents, which may alleviate feelings of being the only stay-at-home mom in your city! On the other hand, a large group will not be as intimate or spontaneous as a small playgroup would be, and the meetings may not fit your schedule.

Also, while most local chapters do sponsor family activities, generally the parents and the children are separated for the regular meetings. You may find this a refreshing and relaxing break, or you may be dismayed at being separated from your child—and your child may feel the same way! If your preschooler already attends a Mom's Day Out or preschool program a few days a week, you may prefer not to be separated for yet another activity.

You may be interested in becoming involved in both a mothers' group and a playgroup. Many organizations offer organized playgroups as a benefit for their members. If the one in your area does not have this service, you may meet other moms there who would want to join you in starting a playgroup.

Existing Playgroups

There may be an existing playgroup in your area already. Check out local churches, libraries, community centers, YMCAs and hospitals in your area because that is where the majority of support groups for parents meet.

Again, joining an existing playgroup means all the legwork has been done for you, and all you have to do is enjoy the benefits. At the same time, however, remember that you may have little or no input in how the playgroup functions, and their meetings may not fit your schedule.

Other Groups

Consider enrolling your children in a preschool dance class, a Mom's Day Out program at your church, a Mommy & Me class at the community center, a preschool gymnastics class through the local YMCA, or a local Kindermusik program. If your personal budget will not allow these activities, many libraries and bookstores offer a free story time for children. During any of these activities, introduce yourself to other parents. You may find out about a local playgroup or you may meet other parents interested in starting one with you. Many times, when an organized program breaks for summer, such as a Mom's Day Out for example, the parents and children make plans to meet regularly until the program resumes in the fall.

Organizations in which you belong may also offer opportunities to find others interested in starting a playgroup. For example, the expectant parents in childbirth classes may welcome a chance to get together with their children once they are born. The way these classes are organized, you should have children very close in age if you use this method. Other examples of groups include your Sunday school class or a professional business association.

Among your friends, you may already know a few at-home parents with children, but they don't know each other. Take the initiative and invite all of them to your house or the park for a playdate. If all goes well, suggest that the group continues on a regular basis.

If none of these options appeal to you, try offering to start a playgroup through an institution or establishment. Perhaps your church or community center would welcome a parent-child program. In this case, the church or community center would provide the necessary resources, and you would organize and lead the group.

Internet Options

Surf the Internet for playgroups. Some web sites offer directories of local playgroups. The most extensive directories on the Internet may be found at OnlinePlaygroup.com and PlaydateConnection.com. Also, many of the national organizations for at-home parents have web sites that list their local chapters.

In addition, most online parenting magazines feature discussion and message boards. Through them, you may find existing playgroups in your area or other parents interested in starting a playgroup.

Posters and Flyers

Post flyers in your community at such locations as churches, libraries, parks, hospitals, pediatricians' offices, grocery stores and your local Chamber of Commerce. Include area businesses frequented by moms such as children's clothing stores and maternity stores. You may want to call the businesses in advance to see if they will allow you to post your flyers and to find out if there are any restrictions or requirements for the posters. You may want to leave a stack of leaflets instead of posters in some locations; many times people will take leaflets but won't copy down a phone number from a poster.

Posters and flyers are not difficult to design, and you don't even need a computer. Put your group's name or just "Neighborhood Playgroup" in large print, followed by the day and time you plan to meet, and a few sentences or phrases describing the group. Remember to include your name and phone number. Appendix A is a sample of a flyer for a neighborhood playgroup.

Advertise

Advertise in your local newspaper. Most local papers have a community calendar section in which they will allow non-profit groups to advertise for free. You may wish to name your group, such as "Mommy & Me" or something catchy, and present yourself as a group. For some ideas for playgroup names, read the chapter on "Choosing a Catchy Name."

A newspaper ad would read something like this: "Mommy & Me playgroup for children 0–3 years old and their mommies meets Wednesdays, 10 a. m. Openings for new members! Call (give your first name and phone number) for details."

Press Releases

Playgroups forming in small towns with newspapers have a better chance at getting photos and press releases printed than playgroups in large cities. During periods of slow news especially, small hometown newspapers actively seek items for their papers, and they are very receptive to including feature stories and photographs about area residents.

Take a photograph of your child playing at the park or doing a craft and write a paragraph about your playgroup. Your photograph does not have to be black and white, but it should be 35 mm and as close to the subject as possible. The photo release can be written as if the playgroup already exists and as if this photo was taken during a playgroup activity; or it could be written saying that this playgroup is forming, with the photo giving an example of an activity that will be provided by the playgroup.

Limit the release to one paragraph, including who, what, where, when, why and how: Who is in the photo (name of the children and name of the playgroup), what they are doing, where they are, when they are doing it, why they are doing it, and how they are doing it, if applicable. Include the contact person (you!) and your phone number for the newspaper as well as for anyone interested in joining the playgroup. This method is also a good idea for publicizing the playgroup and trying to "recruit" new moms.

This photograph, for example, was sent to area newspapers with a release that read:

> Members of the Millbrook Area Playgroup show off the 528 pairs of socks they collected during their "Little Feet for Socks" drive. Because most clothing drives yield such few pairs of

socks, the children canvassed several neighborhoods with their moms to collect socks for "Make a Difference Day" October 24. The enterprising young volunteers, who range in age from five months to eight years old, surpassed their goal of 500 pairs of socks! The donated socks have been delivered to various charitable organizations in the tri-county area.

The release ended with the names of the children and with a phone number so that anyone interested in the playgroup could contact us.

If you plan to start a playgroup that is specialized or out of the ordinary in some way, for example a playgroup for at-home dads or for twins, many newspapers may want to write a feature just on the fact that you are starting this special playgroup. This would apply to a large city paper as well. Again, write a press release explaining your intentions on starting the playgroup, or you can call the newspaper and explain your story idea to the editor.

Of course, everyday activities of your playgroup will make good photo releases; newspapers love pictures of children. Community service projects are ideal "photo ops." Publicize the project in advance to local newspapers and television stations, and you may even receive media coverage during the event or activity. Then, photograph your playgroup doing the project, and send out a release to your local paper afterwards, just as the Millbrook Area Playgroup did with "Little Feet for Socks." Be sure to send the release within one week of the event so it won't be old news.

Word-of-Mouth

Follow up all leads for potential members, especially "friends of friends" you hear are at-home moms. Word-of-mouth is still one of the best ways of finding and starting a playgroup. For example, out of 56 members within five years, 21 members found out about the Millbrook Area Playgroup through word-of-mouth. In addition, when I set out to start a playgroup exclusively for preschool boys, I started by asking everyone in the Millbrook Area Playgroup if they knew of any moms with little boys who may be interested. From only one lead that day, the "Little Buddies" playgroup grew to six little boys within a month, all from word-of-mouth.

For this method to work, you must be assertive. Introduce yourself to other moms at the mall, park, fast food restaurants or even your pediatrician's office. Don't worry about making the first move; it's very likely that the other mom in the park is shyer than you are and would be grateful for your efforts. If your children seem to get along well, suggest that all of you get together another day at the park. Once you have established a relationship with another mom or two, suggest that you work together to start a playgroup. Chances are that they will know one or two other at-home moms who may like to join the group.

In addition, ask your husband to mention playgroup to his co-workers in case some have wives and children at home. Basically, mention playgroup to every person you happen to meet everywhere you go! It may be helpful to keep a few copies of the flyer in your car, so when you tell someone about playgroup you will have a handy sheet they can take home. This will be very convenient, since it will have not only a short description of playgroup but also your phone number on it as well.

Distribute Flyers

Distribute flyers in neighborhoods with small children. Follow these six easy steps and specifically target the neighborhoods you want. This method is the quickest way of starting your own playgroup. For example, out of 56 members within five years, 25 found out about the Millbrook Area Playgroup from flyers we distributed in their neighborhoods. This method requires only a little more investment of your time and money than the other methods.

If you choose this method, use this convenient checklist so you won't forget anything.

1. **Create a flyer, postcard or letter** explaining your intention, similar to the sample Appendix B. Don't forget to include your first name and phone number. Give a two-week deadline in which to respond, just in case a few families are on vacation. That way, you won't have to wonder how long to wait for responses, and if you haven't heard from anyone by the deadline, you'll know that you need to distribute more flyers.

2. **Make copies of your flyer** after you have decided which neighborhoods or streets to canvass and estimated the number of houses. Plan to distribute at least 50 to 75 to start, depending on how many stay-at-home moms you think may live in the area. After the two-week deadline, you may wish to distribute another 50, and so on, until your group has reached the size you want.

3. **Put the flyers on the mailboxes** of either all the houses or just those houses that have children's toys in the yard. The more selective you are, the fewer flyers you will need. Look for toys, strollers, minivans and car seats in vehicles. Please note that Federal Regulations prohibit putting items in a mailbox, so attach the flyer to the outside of the mailbox, such as on the flag. This works best with two people—one person to drive and the other person along to attach the flyers. If you don't have the time to distribute flyers, mail them instead. Just drive through the neighborhood and write down the house numbers and streets. Address the letters to "Resident" or "Neighbor." If you use postcards, the postage is significantly less than the postage for a standard letter. Put all the information in a style similar to a party invitation.

4. **Make a list of callers.** Once the calls come in, remember to write down names, children's names, phone numbers, and the best

days and times for having playgroup. Optional information to ask for would be street addresses and email addresses; these are convenient additions to a membership roster. Keep the list in a handy location, maybe by the phone, so you can add to it as you get more calls. It may be helpful to have an answering machine as well.

5. **Plan to host the first playgroup** in your home once you have decided on a day and time convenient for most of them. Call everyone about the date, time and directions a few days before the playgroup session. That way if you don't reach someone, you still have a day or two in which to keep trying.

6. **Now add your group to the playgroup directories on the Internet,** such as OnlinePlaygroup.com and PlaydateConnection.com. You do not need a web site to add your playgroup. Also, perhaps your hometown has a web site that features local organizations. If so, inquire about adding your playgroup.

Chapter 3

Using the Internet to Help

In this digital age, the Internet can only help any organization; you just need to find specific ways of using it that apply to your situation. You certainly don't need the Internet to enjoy a successful playgroup, nor can an Internet group replace the experience of a real playgroup. However, the Internet can be a valuable tool in many ways, not least of which are for promotion, information, and organization of your playgroup.

Promotion

The most difficult part about organizing a playgroup is getting the word out to potential members about the existence of the playgroup. If you post flyers in local businesses, place ads in the newspaper, invite moms you meet at the park, and distribute flyers in neighborhoods, you can't overlook posting your playgroup on the Internet. Although a neighborhood playgroup cannot be formed solely from the Internet yet, you may reach a few moms who otherwise would not have known about the group. Military families, for example, use the Internet to research the area to which they are about to move. During the two years in which our playgroup has had a web site (www.MillbrookPlaygroup.com), five out of 56 moms found out about the playgroup through the Internet. Granted, that's not a lot of people, but they are five moms who were thrilled to find a playgroup in their small town!

Some web sites offer directories of local playgroups in their region. Two sites, OnlinePlaygroup.com and PlaydateConnection.com, list national and international playgroups. Search their directories for existing playgroups in your area and for other moms who may be looking for a playgroup in your area. Add your playgroup to their directories, and any other directories you may find on the Internet. Perhaps your hometown web site features a listing of local organizations and clubs. Inquire about adding your group. Of course, you don't need a web site in order to post your group with these web sites.

If, however, you decide to design a web site for your playgroup, even better! Visitors to your web site can find out more about your playgroup before they even try out a playgroup session. Remember to put your web site address on any flyers, letters or postcards that you distribute.

Another way to get the word out about your playgroup on the Internet is to visit the web sites of other playgroups listed in the directories, and offer to exchange links with them. In addition, submit your playgroup web site to some of the Internet search engines and directories. Submitting your site is a very easy procedure on most search engines. Simply scan to the bottom of the homepage, click on "Submit Your Site" or "Add a Link" or some similar phrase, and follow the directions. Most search engines require only the URL and your email address, and you're done.

Information

The Internet can also be an information resource. In addition to searching for an existing playgroup in your area, visit other playgroups' web sites and see how these groups function. Perhaps you can borrow some of their good ideas. If you strike up an email correspondence with a mom from one of these playgroups, you can glean even more information from her experiences. Support and encouragement from these seasoned playgroup veterans will be valuable for you as well as your group.

Playgroup web sites are not the only sources for information. Many articles have been written on various aspects of playgroups, children and stay-at-home moms, which can be accessed via the Internet. Some online parenting magazines feature how-to articles, craft ideas, activities for children, and other information you can apply to your playgroup on a regular basis.

The easiest way to find these articles is to use a search engine. Search for "playgroups" as well as other words related to playgroups, and your city and state. Both articles and web sites should come up. Take your time scanning through the list, and visit those that seem appropriate. Once you've read the articles and visited the sites, check out their list of links. The links may lead to you other worthwhile sources.

Online chat groups for at-home moms provide another resource when starting your playgroup. Most online parenting magazines feature discussion and message boards. If you've never checked them out before, you need to! Message boards allow you to post a question or comment and receive input from other stay-at-home parents from all around the nation. Make sure you read the FAQs first before you post a comment. You may also find other stay-at-home parents in your area; message boards are a great start in finding others in similar situations.

You can also use the Internet to find information to jumpstart any activities for your playgroup. For crafts that parents may be interested in, visit CraftCentralStation.com, CraftsFairOnline.com and CraftsInc.com. For children's activities, go to FamilyFun.com, ParentSoup.com and TheIdeaBox.com. Don't forget to check out your hometown web site for information regarding local events and attractions.

OnlinePlaygroup.com offers these resources as well as other valuable services for playgroups of any type. Another notable web site, this one geared specifically for at-home dads and their playgroups, is Slowlane.com.

Organization

The Internet can help you organize your playgroup in various ways. A web site offers a central location for your group to list members, plan activities and post calendars. A web site for a playgroup can almost be synonymous with a newsletter. If your playgroup were to have a newsletter, what would you include? The same would be found on a web site.

A member list would be convenient. No one should have a problem with posting email addresses on the site, but clear it first with your members. However, do not reveal last names, home addresses or phone numbers to maintain their privacy.

Since many people now have family web sites and email photographs to relatives, your members should not object to having the web site feature photos of field trips and other activities from time to time. Our playgroup's web site at MillbrookPlaygroup.com features several photos of our children, and we have never had any problems. However, let your members know that they can contact you if they do not want photographs of their children to be included. As in a newsletter, photographs of events make the web site more interesting. Plus, extended families and playgroup members who may have moved away can now use the web site to keep in touch with members of the group.

A calendar of events keeps busy group members informed. The calendar may include the hostesses for upcoming weekly playgroups as well as information for special events, such as trips to the zoo or picnics at the park or birthday parties.

If your members are scattered in various cities, they may enjoy keeping in touch through a listserv or message board on your web site.

If you think of your web site as an e-newsletter, you can come up with all sorts of additional features your members may use and enjoy. Include favorite recipes, reviews of children's books or movies or toys, lists of special places to take children in your area, simple craft ideas for children, as well as feature articles—written by members!—on family or children topics. Don't forget to list your favorite Internet links!

The Internet provides a wealth of information as well as a vast community of playgroups for those who look for them. Take advantage of it! Use the other at-home moms on the Internet as an ongoing source of support, encouragement and advice. This "virtual group" of moms can be as helpful as the "real" playgroup in your neighborhood, and they are often available to listen at three in the morning!

CHAPTER 4

ORGANIZING AND SETTING GUIDELINES

Although rules and guidelines are not necessary for a successful playgroup, they can be very helpful for even a small group. If you establish guidelines early on, everyone knows what to expect, and new members who join the group later will feel more comfortable. Trying to establish guidelines after the group has been functioning for a while may cause hurt feelings, so at the very first meeting discuss the organization of the playgroup. Now is the time to set rules and guidelines regarding such issues as frequency of meeting, types of activities, discipline, and other expectations of the group. You may want to have a few printed guidelines to pass out at the first meeting to get your group started. The group can decide to make any necessary changes then, or wait until the following meeting.

The larger the group is, the more organization will be needed to keep everything running smoothly. A group numbering more than twelve moms may benefit from having officers, committees and dues. If your group plans many costly activities or field trips, or if you must rent facilities in which to meet, dues may be an essential aid in covering the costs. Determine your expenses before you set the dues. As a result of having membership dues, a treasurer will be needed to handle the finances. Also, an activities coordinator or committee may be beneficial. As a result, a large group may benefit from a set of bylaws rather than simple guidelines. Select a small committee of three to design a draft of bylaws to be discussed with the group as a whole later on and modified if necessary.

A smaller group of twelve moms or less should function just fine without much organization beyond a few guidelines. Guidelines do not have to be elaborate. They are just that—"guides" for the members on how the group will function.

As a matter of fact, the function of the group is a good place to start. If you haven't determined it already, just what is the function of your playgroup? In other words, what is your mission or purpose? Why are you getting together? This was probably determined at the time you decided to start the group, but if not, now is the time to decide that. Is the playgroup designed primarily as a support group for the moms? If so, your guidelines and activities will focus on parental needs. Is the playgroup purely a social group, developed for the social interaction of the children? If so, will the children vary in age and sex, or will they all be toddlers, for example? Various structured activities or no activities at all will be based upon the age range of the youngsters.

The answers to these questions should be reflected in the guidelines. If you're having difficulty determining the answers to these questions, or if you need more help in deciding what you want your playgroup to be, read the chapter "Designing a Playgroup for You and Your Child." Generally, guidelines should cover the following issues:

- Mission or primary function of the group
- Discipline and behavior of the children
- Supervision of the children
- Duties of the hostess
- Membership dues, if any
- Types of structured activities, if any
- Location and any specific rules regarding its use
- Length of playgroup
- Any other expectations of members, such as what to do if you are unable to participate that week

- Extra services and benefits of the playgroup, such as family activities, newsletters and Moms' Night Out
- Duties of officers, if any

Below are five sets of guidelines for playgroups of various sizes. Feel free to use what your group needs, and tailor them for your own playgroup.

Eight to Ten Members

Here is a set of guidelines designed for a free, rotating playgroup of about eight to ten moms.

1. Playgroup is free; all we ask is your participation. Since it is a rotating playgroup, your only obligation is to take your turn hosting playgroup. We follow the phone list for host rotation.

2. Our playgroup is purely a social group, developed for the social interaction of our children. Because of the wide range of our children's ages, structured activities or crafts have proven unfeasible whenever we've tried them in the past.

3. If you or any of your children are sick, or even recovering from an illness, please refrain from participating in playgroup that week. Please contact the host mom if you know you will be unable to attend playgroup, so she can prepare accordingly.

4. As hostess, all you have to do is provide snacks and call everyone the day before to confirm the location. If you need to reschedule your turn to host playgroup, check first with the mom who follows you on the phone list to see if she can switch. If she can't, go to the next mom on the list. When you switch playgroup dates, be sure that you or the new hostess will contact all the moms.

5. You may invite other stay-at-home moms and their children to playgroup at any time. Please contact the hostess in advance so that she can plan accordingly.

6. Although we seldom cancel playgroup, we may skip certain moms in the rotation as necessary. Some moms who may be skipped completely during one or two rotations include new moms to the group, those who are in the last month of pregnancy, moms who have newborn infants, or moms whose families have just had the flu or other contagious illness.

7. The hostess provides a light brunch, such as muffins and fruit.

8. Don't forget to baby-proof your house in case your child hasn't been a baby in a long time.

9. Put away favorite toys so they won't accidentally get broken and so there won't be any conflicts with sharing.

10. Keep the television off so the children will play.

11. Pets should be kept in another room.

12. We try to keep small babies who are on the floor in a safe area of the room where older children will not accidentally bother them. Putting them on a blanket with their toys and telling the other children that area is off limits usually works very well.

13. You are responsible for your child's behavior. If the children are playing in an adjacent room, check on your child frequently. If your child is having a particularly bad day, you may consider removing the child from the play area for a short time, or even leaving early and rejoining playgroup the following week.

14. Please allow each mother to discipline her children in her own manner.

15. Before everyone starts to leave, help your children pick up toys.

Five Members

Here are sample guidelines for a small playgroup of five parents of toddler and preschool boys.

1. Our playgroup is designed for our little boys, ages eighteen months to five years old. Our intention is to keep the group small and intimate so that our sons may develop friendships with other little boys and so that we can manage and supervise structured activities easily. Older and younger siblings are welcome, but they may find the activities unsuited to their tastes.

2. We meet weekly for an hour and a half. Your only obligation is to take your turn hosting the group; the location is up to you.

3. The hostess provides a structured activity or directed play, such as a sandbox, sidewalk chalk, T-ball, water guns and kiddie pool. Notify moms of the activity so that they may dress their sons appropriately.

4. The hostess provides a light snack, such as cookies and drinks.

5. Contact the hostess if you will be unable to attend.

6. Each mom is responsible for her son's behavior. Keep in mind that boys tend to play rough, so try not to overreact to negative behavior.

Eight Members

Here is a set of guidelines for an organization of several playgroups made up of eight moms each.

1. Playgroup is neither a preschool nor a babysitting service. All moms are required to bring their children and stay with them the entire time.

2. Each member will host playgroup once every eight weeks.

3. When hosting you may have playgroup at your home or at another location, such as the park or zoo.

4. If you cannot host on your turn, please choose another location for the group to meet and then notify everyone of the place.

5. When hosting please make sure all members have directions to your home or where you choose for us to meet.

6. Please bring your own snacks to playgroup. The hostess will provide drinks.

7. Please make every effort to let the hostess know each week if you will be able to attend so she can know how many to prepare for.

8. It is not mandatory that you come each week. You may come as often or as little as you choose.

9. If you decide that you will be unable to participate in the playgroup, please contact the Playgroup Coordinator so she can add another to the group. Also, if you decide to change playgroups, please contact the Playgroup Coordinator so we may keep an accurate record of the playgroups.

10. Each playgroup is based on age. Plan for approximately:

    18 months and younger: 1 hour

    19 months to 35 months: 1½ hours

    36 months and older: 2 hours

Large Mothers' Group

A large mothers' group may benefit from bylaws. At the very least, identify the necessary officers and their duties. The following list includes the officers for a large group composed of about fifty families. Your group may need these officers as well, or you may combine two positions into one.

1. All officers serve for one year.

2. The President serves as the leader of the group, arranges for facilities, and organizes guest speakers, lectures, seminars and group discussions.

3.   The Vice President assists the President with organizing the meetings, handles preparations necessary for the children during meetings, and greets new members.

4.   The Secretary keeps up with participation and enrollment, takes the minutes of business meetings, and prepares copies of the minutes for distribution.

5.   The Treasurer manages all finances of the organization.

6.   The Membership Coordinator works closely with the Treasurer to keep track of the status of each member, then compiles, prints and distributes a membership roster.

7.   The Librarian maintains the collection of parenting books and videos.

8.   The Newsletter Editor collects information, designs, prints and distributes a monthly newsletter.

9.   The Webmaster designs and maintains the web site.

10. The Babysitting Co-op/Playgroup Coordinator supervises the services of the co-op and the various playgroups.

11. The Social Activities Coordinator organizes family functions and field trips.

12. The Outreach Coordinator handles publicity for the group to attract new members and organizes community service projects.

For sample bylaws that you can use as a foundation for your bylaws, search the Internet for organizations similar to yours. Contact the leaders for copies of the bylaws and for permission to use them.

Rules for Field Trips

At the very least, your group should agree on standards of behavior for your children, particularly if you plan on going on field trips. Below are some rules you may want to consider.

1. These rules and procedures have been established to prevent hassles and embarrassment, to give our field trip host a reasonably accurate count of people that will be attending, and to observe any rules the host may have.

2. The safety and discipline of the children are the responsibility of the parent or guardian.

3. The person in charge of the field trip has the authority to insist that the parent remove disruptive children.

4. During meetings and special events, such as holiday parties, childcare supervisors will take any discipline matters to the parent of the offending child. At no time do we endorse corporal punishment by the supervisors.

5. Do not bring items that are precious to you or your child. The organization is not responsible for the loss or damage of any personal items.

6. Please let the group leader or person in charge of the field trip know in advance if you plan to attend. If last minute problems occur, call the person in charge as soon as possible.

7. Should an event be cancelled or other problems ensue, you will be contacted as soon as possible via telephone or email. If at all possible, check your email the night before or the morning of the field trip to verify that no one has been trying to reach you.

8. Attend field trips and other group events with your own children or send your children with an adult who will be responsible for their behavior.

9. Arrive on time. We will not wait for latecomers.

10. Children and adults should listen when someone is talking. There are other times better suited for fellowship.

11. Respect age limits. The host sets the age restrictions. Do not bring extra children or babies without first getting permission from the person in charge of the field trip.

12. Be generous with "thank you" and "please."

13. Thank you notes are appropriate. The person in charge of the field trip is responsible for sending a thank you note to the host in a timely manner.

14. Our field trip hosts do not have to provide educational opportunities for our children. Their choice to continue to do so may well be influenced by our behavior.

CHAPTER 5

CHOOSING A CATCHY NAME

Now that your group is organized, make it official. Name your playgroup. Having a name for the group fosters unity among its members. Think what you could do with a name—design cute little T-shirts for the children or make up a signature song! Many newspapers allow free ads for non-profit organizations, and many businesses offer discounts for members of a non-profit organization. So come up with a name and present yourself as an organized group.

Find a name that describes you. If the playgroup is composed of moms and children exclusively from your neighborhood, name your group after the neighborhood. If your members range from one end of the city to the other, you could always name the group after your city, similar to the Millbrook Area Playgroup.

Then again, it could be something catchy and cute! You could come up with an acronym for your group, such as BAMBI for Babies And Mommies of Bloomington, Indiana. If you can't think of an acronym, here are more than 50 other suggestions:

Baby Bunch
Baby Club
Baby Time
Baby Zone
Best Buddies

Busy Babies
Children First
Cutie Pies
Early Birds
First Friends
Fun Friends
Happy Time
Kid Club
Kid Zone
Let's Play
Little Buddies
Little Chicks
Little Friends
Little Ladies
Little Lambs
Little Men
Little Munchkins
Little Ones
Little Pals
Little Rascals
Little Sprouts
Little Tykes
Little Women
Mini Munchkins
Mom-to-Mom
Moms-N-Tots
Moms & More
Mom-N-Kid Club
Moms at Home
Mommy & Me
Mommy Time
Mothers and Babies

Mothers First
Pat-A-Cakes
Perfect Pals
Petite Pals
Playgroup Central
Playgroup Station
Preschool Pals
Preschool Partners
Preschool Playgroup
Preschool Playmates
Saturday Club
Sugar-N-Spice
Sweet Things
Tiny Tots
Tiny Treasures
Tiny Tykes
Toddler Time
Totally Tots
Tot Stop
Tot Time
Wee Ones
Wild Bunch
Wild Things

These are just a few suggestions. The possibilities are limited only by your imagination!

CHAPTER 6

PREPARING TO HOST PLAYGROUP

Okay, you've followed the "Step-by-Step Guide to Starting Your Playgroup." You are expecting anywhere from six to ten moms to show up at your home for your first playgroup meeting. Now what?! Don't panic. This chapter will give you an idea of what to expect at playgroup and how to prepare. These tips will make the playgroup run smoothly and ensure that everyone has a great time from the very first meeting! You will find a convenient checklist at the end of the chapter.

Decisions and Issues

At the first meeting, you may want to discuss such issues as how often the playgroup should meet, whether or not a small membership fee should be charged, whether children will participate in structured activities or just free play, and what discipline policies should be in place. You may find it beneficial from the beginning to establish the rule that if any kids are sick, or even if they are recovering from an illness, they cannot participate in that week's playgroup.

Most playgroups would benefit from instituting guidelines or rules from the very first meeting, rather than try to introduce them later. If possible, have a few guidelines written down, and pass out copies for the members. Any changes can be made today, or you can suggest they look over the list and consider modifications or additions at the next playgroup session.

Finding a convenient day and time to schedule your playgroup is very important to its success. Usually, weekdays are better since most families plan activities for the weekends, and mornings are better because children tend to get cranky in the evenings. However, the best days and times for one playgroup may not be the best for another group. At the first meeting, discuss and agree on the best day and time for your group to meet, and do your best to stick to the schedule. You may be inclined to want to be as flexible as possible so that everyone will be able to attend. Unfortunately, a successful playgroup cannot be that flexible from week to week. A variable meeting schedule can cause confusion, and the playgroup's momentum will be lost.

Set a beginning time and ending time for the playgroup. Generally two hours seem to work best, but consider the ages of the children. Be aware of nap and feeding times, and remember that the younger the children are, the shorter playgroup needs to be.

If your group has ten or fewer moms, you should be able to meet in each other's homes. If your group grows beyond that size, you'll probably need to find a suitable meeting space in a church or community center or to split into two groups. The Millbrook Area Playgroup has continued to meet in each other's homes comfortably with as many as eleven moms and nineteen children. No matter how small a house is, every home has a living room and at least one bedroom for playing. Everyone may not be able to spread out, but a house is never too small. You may want to discuss the issue of location with the other members at the first meeting, either suggesting that the group should meet in a central location or reminding everyone that she will be taking her turn hosting playgroup in her home.

If you meet in a central location, you can take advantage of the extra space by dividing into smaller, more intimate groups. Each group may be based upon the ages of the children involved, particularly if the members participate in structured activities with the children. If the parents generally separate from the children for adult activities, the youngsters can still be divided into smaller groups based on age to make them easier to manage. However, keep in mind that you will need an adequate number of babysitters for each group, and this may pose a financial concern.

You may benefit from nametags if your group is very large. This is a good idea for the first meeting as well as for all the meetings. That way, no one will worry about forgetting someone's name, and it may alleviate some of the awkwardness of attending a function for the first time among people you haven't met yet. There are several nametag kits on the market. If money is an issue, self-adhesive nametags are not very expensive, or you could use index cards and safety pins.

Depending on the size of your group and how your meetings are organized, your children may benefit from nametags as well. Put the children's first names on their tags as well as their parents' names, particularly if the parents and children will be separated during the meeting. That way, if a child becomes upset the babysitter will know whom to ask for in the parent group.

Clearly define the duties of the host mom so that everyone who joins the playgroup will know what to expect. You'll need to decide, for example, whether the hostess is expected to provide a light lunch or just snacks. The time of day that the playgroup meets should help determine the snacks to a degree. A playgroup that meets close to noon may want to share lunch together or may opt for no snacks at all. Remember, however, it is good manners to offer your guests a drink at least.

Before everyone leaves, ask for a volunteer to host next week's playgroup. If you notice any reluctance to volunteer to host the next playgroup, offer your house again. It may take more than one meeting for others to feel comfortable enough to host themselves.

It may be easier to schedule the rotation. Scheduling the next several playgroup dates ensures that everyone knows when she is designated to have it in her home, everyone takes a turn, and no one ends up hosting it too often. Toward the end of the playgroup session, just get out a calendar and start asking everyone what day they want. For those moms who are absent on the day of scheduling, make it a policy that they will be assigned a date after everyone else has chosen. An even better alternative is for the rotation to follow the phone list. Then you won't have to worry about those moms who were absent the day of the scheduling, and it should make it easy for everyone to remember where she is in the rotation. If someone gets an inconvenient date, she can always switch with someone else.

Remind whoever hosts the next playgroup to call the others a day or two beforehand to confirm the location and time. It serves as a reminder to the members who may have had a busy week and lets them know that they won't have to worry about showing up at the home of a mom who forgot she was hosting that week! Also, give directions if necessary.

Preparations for Hosting

If possible, print a list of your playgroup moms, their children's names, addresses and phone numbers to distribute at the first playgroup date. This helps you get to know each other. Update the list periodically as people join and leave.

Put away any items that you may not want little hands to touch.

Don't forget to baby-proof your house in case your child hasn't been a baby in a long time. Cover electrical outlets, remove all breakables, and put gates at stairways.

Just to be on the safe side, have a first aid kit handy.

Pets should be kept in another room during playgroup, unless otherwise agreed to by all members of the playgroup.

If you don't want the children in various rooms in your house, choose a variety of toys and place them in a designated play area. Move furniture around if necessary to create a good play environment. If possible, have places for the moms to sit near the play area. Some playgroups establish a rule early on that the moms and children remain in the same play area so that the moms can supervise their activities and prevent accidents or conflicts. In other playgroups, the children play in a nearby room so there will be less noise in the area where the moms are talking. Either situation may be suitable for your playgroup, but it really depends on the number of children, their ages and temperaments, as well as the desires of the moms.

A big open space is most desirable for a play area. If weather permits, consider having playgroup outside. However, keep in mind that some moms may prefer the safer indoor environment.

If your playgroup engages in structured activities, gather all the necessary items in one location before your guests start arriving.

Greet your guests at the door so that they will feel welcome. This is especially important the first few times a mom and her children have joined playgroup. If the playgroup congregates in the back yard, put a sign on your front door directing any late arrivals to come on in or to go around to the back yard. Especially in a large facility such as a church, post signs in strategic locations giving directions to the rooms your group will be using.

Once your guests have arrived, enjoy yourself! Don't stress out too much on trying to make everything perfect. Playgroup is supposed to be fun, so relax and make new friends!

Snacks

To help break the ice, offer refreshments about a half-hour after everyone has arrived. Snack time is also a good way to divide free playtime and structured activities. Refreshments do not have to be elaborate. Fruit, cookies, chips and drinks or some other combination should suffice.

Keep in mind, however, that some parents do not allow their children to eat sweets between meals. During the first meeting, you may want to offer a variety of refreshments, ranging from healthy snacks such as fruits and bran muffins to sweets such as cookies, so that parents will have a choice for their children. At this time, determine any restrictions regarding snacks as well as any allergies; repeat this process periodically as new moms and children join the playgroup. Remember, it is good manners to offer drinks to your guests, at the very least.

If you serve snacks, consider using paper plates, napkins and cups for easy cleanup. Choose appropriate foods for the age level of the children. All children love cheese puffs, but these snacks can be very messy, and you'll be the one to clean up afterwards! Provide plastic cups with lids and serve colorless juice such as apple to avoid stains. Juice boxes are very convenient, but they can be messy. If a child squeezes the box inadvertently, juice squirts out of the straw.

Provide a bottle of hand sanitizing gel for cleanup before snack time to avoid pile-ups and messes at the sink.

If your kitchen is too small for all the children at snack time and you have to expand to another room, place a tablecloth or sheet on the floor to catch crumbs. This will make cleaning up easier and will provide boundaries for the children.

Format and Structure

Try to keep the playgroup format consistent, so that the children always know what to expect, no matter where the playgroup gathers. This way, moms in the playgroup can take turns hosting without upsetting the children, and the children will feel more comfortable during the playgroup session.

The ideal playgroup will have children who are close in age. Since babies and toddlers are at different stages of development, mixing them can sometimes be difficult. However, age differences sometimes work very well. Babies usually enjoy watching older children play.

If playgroup includes a wide range of ages, try to keep the babies who are on the floor in a safe area of the room where older children won't accidentally bother them. Maybe put them on a blanket with their toys and tell the other children that area is off limits.

Don't worry if you don't have any toys for children over one year of age. Children will find new ways of playing with any kind of toy, even one designed for infants. Or you can resolve the problem by having everyone take a few toys to play with at your house.

If your playgroup engages in structured activities, don't force your child to participate if he doesn't want to. Maybe something else is distracting him or maybe he's just a little shy that day. Gently suggest and encourage him, but don't push him. Remember that your playgroup is not meant to be a preschool, so keep it relaxed and informal.

Prepare your child for playgroup by letting him know what to expect and how to behave. If playgroup will be held in his home, tell him that his little friends are coming over to play with him. Mention some of their names and remind him how much fun he has had with them in the past. If your child has any favorite toys he may not want to share, help him put them away in a safe place, but remind him that he needs to share his other toys. Reassure him that no one will take his toys home. If playgroup will be held in another house, tell him that he will get a chance to play with his little friends and that he will need to share the toys. Reassure him that you will stay there for the entire playgroup session. It is important for your child to feel secure, whether in his own home or in another house, so that he can enjoy the playgroup experience.

If your child is just beginning to potty train, you may want to skip playgroup a time or two. When a child is busy playing, he may have an accident. If you don't want to miss playgroup, consider bringing his portable potty just in case he refuses to use what's available and have an extra set of clothes with you. When you arrive at the location for playgroup, let your child know that a bathroom is available and perhaps ask him periodically if he needs to use it.

Since playgroup is time for the children to play together and interact socially, keep the television off. On the other hand, movie time could be an effective way to calm children down if things start getting out of hand. The hostess might have a child's movie on hand just in case it's needed. However, since child-to-child interaction is low during movies, just be careful to limit the movie time as much as possible.

Behavior and Discipline

You are responsible for your child's behavior, so be alert and focus on your children and their interaction with others. At the same time, try not to overreact to your child or another child's negative behavior. Conflicts are likely to occur from time to time.

There are two types of children you will find in almost any playgroup. If you are prepared, you can handle them and reassure the parents. The first is the child who clings to her mom and seems a bit overwhelmed by the children. A little more reserved than her companions, she sits back on her mom's lap and observes the other children for a while. Don't worry; she just needs some time to check things out. She'll probably warm up to the group and join right in after a few weeks.

The second type of child is one our playgroup refers to as the "wild child." Usually a boy between the ages of two and three-and-a-half, this child is active, energetic, loud, and into everything. He often plays rough, may not like to share, and will aggressively defend his toys and territory. Again, don't worry; there's not much you can do except keep an eye on him so he won't hurt the other children and then wait out this phase. Soon after he is three-and-a-half, he will have calmed down considerably. If his mother will watch him to prevent accidents from happening and to reprimand him as needed, the other moms will not develop resentment towards the child and his mom. Remember, there is nothing worse than having your child hurt by another child and having that child's mother do nothing about it.

Avoid making comparisons among the children.

Remember that two-year-old children will usually be involved in parallel play, where they will play with toys and activities next to each other and seldom interact. Three-year-olds are only beginning to play together. By the time they are four, children are finally role-playing and using more imagination as they play with other children. Learning to share is something that takes time and experience. A playgroup is an excellent environment in which to do that.

Each mother is responsible for the discipline of her own children. If your child is having a particularly bad day, you may consider removing the child from the play area for a short time, or even leaving early and rejoining playgroup the following week.

At the end of playgroup, praise those children who were particularly well behaved, especially if they are generally a handful! Positive reinforcement goes a long way to establishing the kind of behavior you want.

Cleaning Up

Before everyone starts to leave, help your children pick up toys or clean up from the craft. They will be more inclined to do their share if their moms are helping. Make it fun! Perhaps sing the "Clean Up" song as you pick up toys, starting off slow and getting faster and faster. The words to the song are: "Clean up, clean up, everybody everywhere! Clean up, clean up, everybody do your share!" Or tell each child to pick up a certain number of toys, fifteen for example, and help your child count each toy until he reaches the goal.

Also, help clean up from snack time. You'll want the other moms to return the favor when you host playgroup in your home!

Consider ending your playgroup with a goodbye song to help the children transition out of playgroup smoothly. Maybe sing the song right after you finish picking up toys. Make up your own goodbye song, or use one that the children already like. If the moms aren't already burned out on Barney's "I Love You, You Love Me," let that be your goodbye song. Another suggestion may be the "ABC Song," ending with "Now I've sung my ABC's/It's time to say goodbye to me!" Here is another cute song with movements. Replace "everybody" with your group's name:

> Everybody turn around (turn around once),
> Everybody touch the ground (bend over and touch the floor with your fingers),
> Everybody reach up high (stretch your arms above your head),
> Everybody say "Bye-bye!" (use both hands to wave good-bye)

As you are leaving, don't forget to thank your hostess for opening her home to the playgroup.

Just as a preventive measure, once everyone has left your house or once you have gotten home from playgroup, wash your hands and your children's hands as well. This will prevent many illnesses.

The Second Meeting and Beyond

Most likely, expect everyone who indicated an interest in playgroup to attend the first session, although attendance will then drop off for a few sessions. This is normal. The members may have prior commitments they couldn't change, or they could have forgotten about playgroup. This is why it is important to call members a day or two before each playgroup session to remind them and to give directions if necessary. Generally, though, it just takes a few weeks for playgroup to become a habit and for attendance to remain steady. After three sessions, your playgroup should be well on the way to being an established organization.

Expect nearly everyone to arrive on time for the first session of playgroup. For subsequent sessions, however, you may find that nearly everyone arrives between fifteen and thirty minutes after the official start of playgroup. This is normal, as the members are growing comfortable with the group. Besides, we all know how difficult it sometimes is to arrive anywhere on time with children in tow! If latecomers are causing problems, consider changing the starting time for playgroup to fifteen or thirty minutes later.

Although playgroup will generally end on time, you can expect some moms to linger occasionally, especially if they are having a good time. As a matter of fact, if you still have guests in your house up to thirty minutes past the official end of playgroup, consider it a compliment. They are enjoying themselves so much that they don't want to leave! However, if members consistently linger week after week, perhaps your playgroup is not long enough. Consider extending it to two hours. On the other hand, if the group must end by a certain time, take the initiative by starting to pick up toys or helping to clean up about fifteen minutes before playgroup officially should end. The other members should take the hint and respond accordingly.

Convenient Checklist for Playgroup Hostess

1. Call all members the day before playgroup.
2. Provide copies of suggested guidelines (for first meeting).
3. Prepare updated copies of your Membership List, if necessary.
4. Offer appropriate snacks and beverages, with "sippy" cups if necessary.

5. Ensure adequate number of plates, napkins and cups.

6. Have a first aid kit and a bottle of hand sanitizing gel.

7. Put away favorite toys and breakable items.

8. Baby-proof the areas of the house where playgroup will gather.

9. Confine pets in a room or outside.

10. Prepare play area by setting out toys and moving furniture if necessary.

11. Gather supplies for the structured activity, if necessary.

12. Turn the television off.

13. Prepare your child for guests.

CHAPTER 7

INCLUDING PARENTS IN ON THE FUN

Playgroups provide peer groups for moms and kids as well as time to get out of the house and something to look forward to later in the week. Your playgroup can be a forum for discussion, a place to do fun crafts, or a time to share activities with your child.

But there can be more! Depending on the size of your playgroup, you can offer benefits and services just for the parents, ranging from a monthly newsletter to a moms' night out, from a babysitting co-op to a recipe exchange. Use these suggestions to make your playgroup exactly what you want it to be, and you'll find that the parents enjoy playgroup as much as their children do!

Help During Personal Need

As a support system for moms, the playgroup is unmatched, especially for families who do not have relatives nearby. In times of personal need, the moms from playgroup can pitch in to help. For example, a mom who has just had a second baby may appreciate a few meals brought over for her family so she won't have to cook. Arrange for each mom in playgroup to have a night in which she prepares a meal for the new mom and her family. Those who feel inadequate in the kitchen can pair with another mom who brings the entrée while she contributes a side dish or dessert.

In dealing with an emergency for one child, a mom may need a babysitter for her other child in a pinch. Sometimes a mom may need a safe place for her child when she herself is ill. Some playgroups institute an "In a Pinch" service with a list of moms who can babysit at the last minute. At the very least, a supportive phone call in a stressful day can keep a harried mom from becoming too frustrated. With a playgroup phone list, she can pick up the phone and call a playgroup mom for a little "time out" and encouragement.

For many women living far away from relatives, the moms in playgroup provide the support that the extended family used to provide in times past. When one of your members is in need, organize help. At the same time, if you are in need, don't hesitate to call on a playgroup member. That's what friends are for!

Secret Pals

Bring your members closer and add a little fun at the same time with secret pals. In this program, each of you will have another parent in the group to whom you secretly send cards and small gifts during the year. You don't find out who your secret pal is until the end of the year. If your membership fluctuates too much to maintain secret pals for a year, institute it for only a quarter at a time.

Care Groups

For a large mothers' group, consider forming care groups. These are smaller groups of moms specifically designed to provide help and support when needed. It's easy for one mom to get lost in the shuffle of a large organization with many members. In smaller care groups, the members would be more likely to be aware of the potential needs of the others in their group and would be more likely to volunteer when the need arises.

Favor Exchange

You may need a favor and don't know who to ask or how to go about asking. Many times it's easier to ask a group of people for a favor and get a volunteer, than to ask someone directly. That's what you get with a favor exchange, and all you have to do is be available to do a favor for someone else in playgroup in return. Some favors are needed during vacations, such as house sitting and pet sitting. Other times you just need a helping hand, such as a ride to the airport. Someone in charge of the favor exchange keeps up with the list of favors and calls volunteers.

Informal Clubs and Hobbies

All parents in playgroups have at least one thing in common: Children. But you may find that you have other interests in common as you get to know each other. Take this opportunity to spend time outside of playgroup with others who share your interests or hobbies. Perhaps start an informal club for scrapbooking, join an aerobics class together, form a bowling league, or meet for games of tennis. The important thing is to nurture the friendships you are forming in playgroup.

Barter Your Skills

A playgroup offers an opportunity to share your expertise, whatever it may be. For example, the gardener among you could arrange to organize those moms who need help starting a vegetable garden or planting flowers and shrubs. All of the moms share the work, with one mom to babysit, while the expert directs the operation and supervises. This way, all those involved get beautiful flowerbeds without having to do all the work themselves. Through the years, the members of the Millbrook Area Playgroup have planted flowerbeds, redecorated various rooms in their homes, and accomplished many other big projects this way!

Another way to share skills in the group is to barter. For example, three moms with skills in playing the piano, watercolor painting or using the computer could gather once a week or twice a month for lessons. The lessons could be for the children or for the adults too.

Babysitting Co-op

Some moms share in a babysitting co-op where they take turns babysitting each other's children on a regular basis. One mom keeps the children on one day while the other mom enjoys her free time, and then they switch on another day that week or the following week. The co-op could even be used for weekends so parents could go out without the hassle of finding a sitter and the expense of paying for one. The parents feel more comfortable knowing their children are watched by an adult they know and by someone with whom the children feel comfortable.

Babysitting co-ops work best with moms who have the same number of children, but you can develop a system to accommodate a mom with one child and another mom with three children. Perhaps the mom with one child gets an extra hour on her free day. Or you could develop a point system per child where the moms collect points that they can cash in as they need them.

Moms' Night Out

Organize a moms' night out periodically where the moms get together to eat dinner at a local restaurant or to see a movie without the children. Arrange the outing on a night when all the fathers can be home with the children, or find babysitters to share. Imagine a relaxing meal among adults, without preschoolers to take to the restroom, toddlers to entertain, or babies to feed! These nights out give the moms time off from family responsibilities and a chance to interact with other at-home parents in a relaxed setting.

Some playgroups go all out and arrange a moms' weekend retreat. These can be as simple or as elaborate as expenses and desires allow, from a simple weekend at the beach to a series of lectures and workshops by guest speakers.

Project Night

Many playgroups institute a project night once a month. Usually hosted by a different mom each time, a project night gives moms a chance to work on their own hobbies or projects as they talk and socialize with each other. For example, moms may work on a scrapbook, finish a needlepoint project, or paint their nails—any project they need to do but can't find the time to do at home. During the holidays, it may turn into a gift-wrapping session.

Family Socials

Organize family functions that include spouses and older children so you can all get to know each other. Gather at the local park for a picnic or at a member's home for a pool party, a potluck supper, or game night. Attend a sports event together or organize a campout for the dads and children in a member's backyard. Holiday parties are another way of including the whole family.

Couples' Night Out

For activities without the children, institute a couples' night out. The group could pitch in to hire a babysitter or two in one location and enjoy dinner at a local restaurant or a movie together. Alternatively, playgroup members could rotate babysitting duties. Of course, both parents must agree to this option, so that when it is their turn to watch the children the supervision is shared. Otherwise, only one parent will be in charge of all the children, which may be too much work for one person.

Playgroup Baby Shower

Is there a mom in the group who's expecting a second child? Organize a playgroup baby shower during a regularly scheduled play-group session. Additional friends of the expectant mother may be invited, but it's sure to be a convenient time for nearly everyone in your playgroup! Playgroup baby showers provide an excellent opportunity for all members to pitch in for that one expensive gift the new mom wants. Since most families save baby items from their first child, you won't have to worry about duplicating something they already have.

Goodbye Playgroup

Say goodbye as a group to those members who must move away, especially if they have been actively involved with playgroup for a while. Throw a goodbye party during their last playgroup session, perhaps with a cake and a small gift such as a framed photo of playgroup. Don't forget some little token for the children as well, such as a stuffed animal or other toy. Be sure the parents leave with a playgroup list so they can contact you when they have settled in their new home!

Special Speakers

Schedule a special lecture during playgroup. The children may have to be supervised in a separate room or in the backyard, but the moms may enjoy an informative lecture related to home and family or health and fitness. To avoid having to pay a speaker's fees, each mom in your group may be an "expert" on some topic or may have a friend who would be willing to speak for free; otherwise, membership dues or donations can cover the cost.

After the speaker concludes, break into smaller groups to discuss the topic in depth. Everyone then gets a chance to contribute to the issue, giving examples or sharing experiences. Remember to send a thank you card to your guest speaker afterwards.

Book Discussion

Schedule book discussions during an occasional playgroup session. Each member reads a book previously selected by the group, and everyone discusses it during playgroup. Generally, the selected books deal with child development or some other parenting issue, but this doesn't always have to be the case.

Crafts

Adults enjoy crafts as much as children do! Many women appreciate learning how to make floral arrangements, how to do scrapbooking, or how to make creative gifts. The Internet has a wealth of web sites devoted to crafts. Go to CraftsFairOnline.com, CraftCentralStation.com, and CraftsInc.com to get you started with ideas and directions for all sorts of projects. In addition, you should be able to find a number of books at your local library and bookstore. Your group needs to decide if the hostess will provide the craft supplies each week, if each adult will bring her own materials, or if membership dues will cover the cost of supplies.

Special Activities

Your playgroup can offer various special activities during the meetings. Make your group a "Walking Playgroup," where you take turns walking in each other's neighborhood or at the park. Coffee lovers would enjoy a "Coffee Chat," where each week would mean a different flavor of coffee. The moms would talk and enjoy their coffee while the children play.

Recipe Exchange

Do a recipe exchange occasionally during playgroup. These can be your favorite recipes of any type, or you can specify that they be recipes for desserts or casseroles or holiday treats only. You could even have everyone bring tasty samples of their recipes.

Meal Exchange

A meal exchange is fun if most of the families are the same size and require the same amount of food. Here is what you do. If there are five who want to participate, each one cooks five meals, such as five lasagnas or five casseroles. On the day of the meal exchange, each mom takes four of her meals to playgroup; one meal stays at home for her own family. It works best if the playgroup hostess that week has a large freezer! After playgroup, each mom takes home four different meals for her family, one from each mom who participated. Make sure you find out if there are any allergies or dislikes first!

Bulk Cooking

Bulk cooking is a marathon cooking session at one member's house. The length of time varies depending on how many meals you cook, how many moms help out, and how much time you have, but generally prepare for three to six hours. You need at least three participating moms to facilitate the best use of time and manpower. The best situation provides for at least two cooks and one to help where needed. On a weekday, you may need an extra mom to babysit all the children, but on the weekend you may be able to leave the children with their dads.

Ahead of time, decide on the meals to be cooked and split up the shopping into categories, so that each person has only a part of the shopping to do. Each person can donate incidentals, such as spices and flour. Plan to cook about six meals. With bulk cooking, everyone shares in the cost and preparation, and the average cost per meal is minimal.

Clothing Swap

A clothing swap can be limited to playgroup members or extended to the community at large. Generally, the number and type of clothing items a mother brings to the swap determines the number and type she gets to take home, but the clothing swap can get as organized as you want it to be. Some playgroups simply prefer handing down their outgrown children's clothes to younger children, without exchange or compensation. Clothing swaps can really help families on a one-income budget, even if the clothes are so worn out they need to be restricted to play clothes only.

The swap does not have to be limited to children's clothes, either. Include adult clothing, especially maternity clothes, as well as infant toys or baby items such as swings and car seats.

Share and Borrow

Having a playgroup can almost be like having an extended family, particularly if you need to borrow things that you don't have. For example, if relatives are coming for an extended visit, you may be able to borrow a rollaway bed or portable crib from someone in playgroup.

Also, everyone in playgroup may pitch in for one big item to share. For example, those who wanted to could pool their resources to purchase a carpet cleaner. Whoever needs the carpet cleaner would use it and store it in her home until the next playgroup member needed it. If it gets broken, the one who was using it at the time would pay for one-third of the repair bill, the one who used it before her would pay for one-third and the final one-third would be divided among the other playgroup members who share the cleaner. This way, the repair bill would not be too much for one family on a limited budget, the one who "broke" it would still have more to pay than the others, and the one before her would be sure to keep it in excellent shape until she passed it on. Alternatively, the repairs could be provided for in a fund kept by one person; each time someone uses the cleaner, they pay a small fee that would be kept in this repair fund until needed. That way, those who use the cleaner more frequently would be contributing more to its maintenance. If the repair bill ends up being more than the fund, the person who broke the machine would make up the difference.

Yard Sale

Organize a playgroup yard sale. Pick a Saturday convenient for everyone, and choose a member's house that is located near a busy street. Each mom who participates needs to tag all of her items with the price and her initials. If any initials are duplicated, come up with an alternative for those members. Place an ad in the classified section of the newspaper and post signs around the community. Be sure to emphasize that it is a multi-family yard sale to attract the most customers. The morning of the yard sale you may need to put up signs giving directions to the house to draw passersby.

During the yard sale, delegate the jobs. For example, have one person in charge of the clothes, another in charge of toys, etc., in case a customer needs any help. Designate one person as the "cashier" in charge of the money and have her carry a notepad and pen with her at all times. The notepad should have every participating member's name on a separate page. When an item is bought, the cashier checks the price and the initials on the tag. She receives the money and marks the item's amount under the appropriate member's initials in the notepad. This way, at the end of the yard sale, each member will know how much of the total amount is hers. Box up the leftover items and donate them to a local charity.

If your playgroup is primarily a neighborhood playgroup, include the entire community in the yard sale and just have everyone display their items in their own front yards. Distribute flyers two weeks in advance to notify your neighbors of the pending neighborhood yard sale and to invite them to arrange a sale in their yard that day as well. A neighborhood yard sale attracts larger numbers of customers, and everyone in the area benefits from the advertising. Remember to place the newspaper ads and posters as well as signs giving directions if necessary.

Discounts

Many businesses offer discounts for non-profit organizations. Inquire with various local businesses to see if they will offer such a service for your playgroup.

Calendar

A monthly or quarterly calendar of events is a great way to keep playgroup members together if you don't meet very frequently, if the group is very large, or if you live far apart from each other in a large city or in neighboring towns. It serves as an excellent reminder for upcoming events and activities, especially if the group meets at various locations around the area and enjoys very many pursuits together in addition to playgroup. However, if your group generally meets in your homes and seldom schedules other events, the calendar may not be right for you. For example, if your members need to switch hosting duties sometimes for various reasons, your calendar will be useless. The Millbrook Area Playgroup does not print a calendar for this very reason, but many larger groups find it very helpful.

Print your calendars monthly or quarterly to save money. The cost will be minimal, especially if you hand out the calendars rather than mail them each time, so membership dues or donations should cover the cost if the leader cannot afford it.

Newsletter

In addition to or instead of a calendar, a newsletter is another way to keep your members connected. Not only does it serve as a reminder for upcoming events and activities, but it can also be used as a method for disseminating news and a forum for discussions of child development and parenting issues. A newsletter doesn't have to be elaborate with lots of graphics or photos. To start, simply include a list of your members, calendar of special events, schedule of playgroup locations, and descriptions of what happened at recent events. Later you could add favorite recipes, reviews of children's books or movies or toys, and rainy day activities for children. Encourage parents and children to submit items, such as articles or poems or pictures.

Membership dues or donations should cover the cost of printing and mailing a newsletter.

Web Site

For families online, a web site offers a central location for your group to list members, plan activities and post calendars. If you think of your web site as an e-newsletter, you can come up with all sorts of additional features your members may use and enjoy. Include favorite recipes, quick snack ideas, reviews of children's books or movies or toys, lists of special places to take children in your area, simple craft ideas for children, parenting tips as well as feature articles—written by members—on child development and parenting issues. Don't forget to list your favorite Internet links! Remember, do not refer to last names, addresses or phone numbers on your web site, and check with members first before posting photographs of the children.

Membership dues or donations should cover the cost of web site hosting, although several Internet companies provide web space and hosting for free. Search for them on the Internet. As a matter of fact, OnlinePlaygroup.com offers various ways for playgroups to make the most of the Internet. Check it out!

Email

A web site is not the only way to reach your members over the Internet. Many individuals now have email addresses and go online frequently. Keep in contact with your members through email. With email, they can respond when it's convenient for them, and you can eliminate any long distance phone charges that may apply. Email your members to remind them about upcoming events and to follow up on any missed playgroup sessions. It's often quicker and easier than picking up the phone! Just get their email addresses when you get their other information, and make sure it all remains confidential.

Phone Tree

A phone tree is essential to keeping a large group connected. With a phone tree, information gets disseminated to every member quickly and easily without having to make very many phone calls and without long distance charges. The phone tree begins with about four members, each of whom have only three or four other members to have to call; then those three or four have three or four others, and so on.

CHAPTER 8

MAKING PLAYGROUP FUN FOR KIDS

Some playgroups provide structured activities for the children, while others remain strictly social playtimes, particularly if the children range in age from infants to preschoolers. The Millbrook Area Playgroup, for example, is a social playgroup by design; the parents talk while the children play. Nevertheless, whether with structured activities or without them, a successful playgroup provides a variety of fun things to do, both during playgroup and between sessions.

Playdates

One benefit of a playgroup is having friends you can call over to play one afternoon. If your child finds a best buddy in playgroup, or if you and another mom hit it off, nurture this new friendship. Schedule a playdate with them. Invite them over one afternoon to play or ask them to join you at the mall. Children often make their first friends in playgroup; they grow up together and even start school in the same classes together.

Impromptu Gatherings

If you, another mom and your children spontaneously get together one morning or afternoon, consider calling a few of the other moms to join you. These impromptu gatherings can be a treat for both children and moms, especially for those new to the group. The new mom may still feel a little like an outsider, despite your best efforts at including her in conversations. Receiving an invitation to join you and a few others during a spontaneous playdate would go a long way to making her feel accepted and excited about playgroup. Plus, it will give the children as well as the adults an opportunity to get to know each other better.

Lunch Bunch

Children enjoy going out for lunch! So do their moms! Gather a group together for a lunch bunch. Nearly all fast food restaurants have play areas attached, and some are even indoors in a climate-controlled environment.

Your lunch bunch doesn't have to meet always at a fast food restaurant. Find an establishment that's child-friendly. Perhaps a restaurant featuring a buffet would be best so that the children won't have to wait for their food. Two to four moms and their children from the Millbrook Area Playgroup have patronized a local Chinese restaurant nearly every Wednesday for its lunch buffet. It is a wonderful change for all of us, plus the buffet always features a few "American" items for those of us with finicky children.

For a large group, consider making reservations ahead of time to reserve a section of the dining room. Please remember to tip your server generously!

Community Service Project

Organize a community service project in which the children can become involved. This could be an annual event or a regular monthly activity. For example, organize a fundraiser for a local charity or decorate a local retirement home for the holidays. You could also visit the elderly, collect your children's outgrown clothing for a local outreach program, or volunteer to deliver meals to the homebound. Not only would you be serving your community, but also your children would benefit from participating in your efforts. Your actions will go a long way in teaching your children the importance of community service and the satisfaction of helping others.

Structured Activities

All children enjoy free playtime during playgroup because it gives them the opportunity to explore and do things on their own. They learn to share, take turns and role-play. On the other hand, structured activities offer a delightful change for many children who are used to playing on their own at home. Your playgroup doesn't necessarily have to be one or the other. Combine the two during one playgroup session, or alternate between free playtime one week and a structured activity or craft the next week.

In advance, your group needs to decide if the hostess will provide the craft supplies each week, if each parent will bring the materials for her children, or if membership dues will cover the cost of supplies.

Circle Time

The activities in a circle time generally appeal to all ages and can be adapted for infants, toddlers and preschoolers. The moms and children literally form a circle in which they tell stories and sing songs. In many playgroups, the circle time is the only structured activity during the session. It either begins or ends playgroup, and is joined by snack time and free playtime.

Don't force your children to join circle time; when they see that the other children enjoy it, they will join in when they are ready and comfortable.

Suggested Activities

The children's section of the bookstore features many books on fun children's activities. Check them out! The Internet, as well, has a wealth of web sites with great ideas for activities and crafts based on age and ability. Go to TheIdeaBox.com, ParentSoup.com, and FamilyFun.com. Basically, though, if your playgroup plans activities for the little participants rather than free play time, here are a few ideas to get you started, based on age. If you want details on these activities, read the chapter titled "Week-by-Week Guide to Children's Activities."

Keep in mind that the average child's attention span on any one activity, whether a craft or game, is about ten minutes! As a result, it may be a good idea to combine several activities during one playgroup session or start playgroup with one activity and end with free playtime. Also, keep in mind that the playgroup is not meant to be a preschool, so keep any structured activities relaxed and informal. These ideas include structured activities, directed play and circle time for various age groups.

- **Infants**—practicing gross motor movement, doing finger plays like "Itsy Bitsy Spider" and "Pat-a-Cake," going for stroller rides around the block or in the park or at the mall, reciting nursery rhymes to them, bringing out various objects for them to touch and feel, reading simple story books to them, rolling a ball, stacking blocks and knocking them down, naming body parts, filling and emptying containers, nesting toys, putting together simple 4-piece puzzles.

- **Toddlers**—doing finger plays together like "Itsy Bitsy Spider" and "Pat-a-Cake," going for stroller rides around the block or in the park or at the mall, singing songs together, reciting nursery rhymes together, dancing, reading stories aloud, finding shapes around the house, counting and sorting objects, coloring, swinging, playing in the sandbox, rolling a ball, putting together simple 10-piece puzzles, pulling and pushing toys with wheels, cuddling and "parenting" soft animals and dolls, making things out of play-doh, blowing bubbles, drawing with sidewalk chalk, building with blocks or Legos or Duplos, playing with dominoes, playing games such as "Duck Duck Goose," splashing in a kiddie pool.

- **Preschoolers**—riding tricycles or big wheels around the neighborhood or in the park, doing finger plays together, singing songs together, reciting nursery rhymes, dancing, reading stories, finding shapes, counting and sorting objects, coloring, putting together simple 20-piece puzzles, swinging, playing in the sandbox, rolling a ball, T-ball, playing house with dolls, doing simple crafts involving cutting and pasting, finger painting, making things out of play-doh, doing tumbling exercises, racing in relays, blowing bubbles, drawing with sidewalk chalk, building with blocks or Legos or Duplos, playing with dominoes, playing games such as "I Spy" or "Duck Duck Goose" or musical chairs, baking cookies or muffins, splashing in a kiddie pool.

Different Locations

Take advantage of those months with mild climates and meet at a local park or playground for playgroup a few times. Everyone can bring a snack or beverage, and no one has to clean her house! Other locations to consider include the beach, lake, zoo, amusement park, mall, arcade, water park, and museum. Depending on the children's ages, you could also take them bowling, roller skating and swimming for an interesting change. Find out what your hometown has to offer.

Field Trips

Take the children on a "field trip" to the zoo, movies, or a children's museum. Check out local businesses to see if they offer "behind the scenes" tours. Other suggestions for field trips that particularly appeal to children are fire stations, police stations, airports, bakeries, ice cream shops, bookstores, and farms. Make the outing age appropriate and remember to send a thank you card afterwards.

Holiday Playgroup

It's fun sometimes to have special holiday playgroups. For example, exchange valentines the week of Valentine's Day, have an Easter egg hunt during the week of Easter, dress up for Halloween, and exchange gifts at Christmas time. A little variety goes a long way to making the playgroup fun for everyone.

Playgroup Themes

Having themes for your playgroup is another delightful way to add variety. For example, have a "blue day" where everyone wears blue or a "pet day" where everyone brings a pet.

Birthday Playgroup

If you plan ahead, a mom can host playgroup the week of her child's birthday, especially if the birthday party would be composed mostly of playgroup children anyway. That way, the mom gets her turn out of the way, the extra costs of two separate events are eliminated, and you don't have to worry about someone unable to attend because of a weekend family conflict. A playgroup birthday party can be as much like a regular playgroup session as you want it to be, just playing as usual with cake and ice cream instead of snacks. The only difference would be opening presents. You can always get more elaborate with a pinata or pony rides, etc.

If your playgroup has several children born in the same month, you may consider combining their parties into one. This will eliminate the impression that playgroup is one birthday party after another for any new moms who may join that month, as well as the expense for members of buying several birthday gifts in a row. This is especially recommended for large mothers' groups. Usually, gifts are not expected at group birthday parties, but all members should agree to this before instituting monthly group birthdays. Alternatively, every playgroup member could pitch in to provide one gift per birthday child, so the birthday children will have something to open at the party.

Birthdays of adults may be commemorated in the same fashion. However, most playgroup parents prefer to celebrate their birthdays with a special Moms' Night Out, a birthday song from the children during playgroup, or just a thoughtful card signed by all the playgroup members.

CHAPTER 9

WEEK-BY-WEEK GUIDE OF CHILDREN'S ACTIVITIES

Here are enough crafts, games, songs and activities to keep your playgroup busy for a whole year! Each week of the year features a different idea with listed necessary items and detailed directions. All materials needed for each activity are common items generally found in most homes. They may not be in every home, but surely, out of your entire playgroup, one mom will have them. Just make sure she hosts that week!

Generally, outdoor activities in this guide are planned for late spring, summer and early fall, while mainly indoor activities are scheduled during winter months. Special activities with holiday themes are arranged for some of the holidays. Most of these ideas appeal to children between the ages of twenty months and five years old. However, you may need to alter them slightly depending on the exact ages of your children, their abilities, and the number in the group. You don't have to limit your playgroup to just these suggestions. If you think something won't work for your group, go to TheIdeaBox.com, ParentSoup.com or FamilyFun.com for excellent suggestions and directions for various activities, games and crafts.

Keep in mind that the average child's attention span on any one activity is about ten to fifteen minutes! Not all of these activities will last a full hour. As a result, it may be a good idea to start playgroup with a structured activity and end with free playtime. Also, keep in mind that the playgroup is not meant to be a preschool, so keep it relaxed and informal. Whatever you decide to do during playgroup, it should be a fun and relaxing time for parents and children, so don't force children to participate if they don't want to. Something else may be attracting their attention or they may be a little shy that day. Don't push them and don't stress out about it either! As long as everyone is having fun, your playgroup will be successful.

January

Week 1—New Year's Day Crown

Items Needed: Construction paper, scissors, glue, stapler, pipe cleaners, glitter, confetti

Directions: Wrap the construction paper around your child's head to find out what size to cut out a "crown" to fit. Then from another piece of construction paper, cut out squares with the numbers for the New Year, cover them with glue and add glitter. Glue pieces of confetti all over the crown. Attach the numbers to the pipe cleaners and attach to the crown. Measure the band to the child's head and then staple the ends together to secure the crown.

Week 2—Paper Bag Puppets

Items Needed: Small paper bags, markers, glue, construction paper cut in shapes of ears, tongue, hair, arms and hands, teeth, plus circles for eyes and noses

Directions: Ahead of time, cut out funny ears, tongues, arms and hands, and hair from construction paper. Have the children glue the parts onto the bag, using the folded section of the paper bag as the face. Now you can put on a puppet show!

Week 3—Story Time Share

Items Needed: Favorite story books, paper, crayons

Directions: Have the children bring their favorite books, one each. Read them to the group. Afterwards, let the children draw and color.

Week 4—Indoor Obstacle Course

Items Needed: Pillows, sofa, chairs, tables (whatever you have in your house)

Directions: Set up an "obstacle course" for the children, where they will climb over sofas, squeeze through chairs, crawl under tables, and roll over pillows. Make sure they take off their shoes first! This could be designed as a "Follow the Leader" game, as a race, or just for fun.

February

Week 1—Scavenger Hunt

Items Needed: Various items in all shapes and colors that children can touch

Directions: List ahead of time the items the children must find. Have them search for things in the shapes of triangles, squares, rectangles, and circles; items in particular colors; or things with specific textures such as soft or smooth; and combinations of all of them. Either they can point items out and see how many they can find, or they can take one item of each description to a central location. You can time the event like a race or you can all work together as a group to find the items.

Week 2—Valentine's Day—Valentines on Construction Paper

Items Needed:Construction paper cut in the shape of a heart, glue, buttons, beads, and other small items to glue, or markers or crayons.

Directions: Each child decorates a heart by gluing on small items or by coloring designs with markers or crayons.

Week 3—Musical Instruments

Items Needed: Two Styrofoam or paper plates per child or an empty canister with a plastic lid, construction paper, masking tape or stapler, glue, paper ribbons, markers or crayons, pebbles or pasta or beans

Directions: For a tambourine, have each child decorate the backs of two Styrofoam or paper plates. Put pebbles, pasta or beans in one plate. Set the other plate on top with the insides facing each other. Attach the two plates together by taping or stapling along the outside rim. Staple or glue ribbons along the edge to hang down like streamers.

For a drum, cut construction paper to fit around the outside of an empty canister. Have the child decorate the construction paper by coloring or gluing items to it. Wrap the finished design around the canister and glue in place. Put the lid on.

Now have the children play in the orchestra!

Week 4—Simon Says

Items Needed: Nothing

Directions: Have a parent be "Simon" first and explain the rules to the children. Have Simon "say" three or four things in a row before the trick command. Have the children touch or shake their toes, feet, knees, tummy, shoulders, chins, necks, heads, as well as have them clap, stomp, jump, hop on one foot, and run in place. Start off slow. As they get used to the game, you can get faster.

March

Week 1—Paper Roll Binoculars

Items Needed: Two empty toilet paper rolls or one empty paper towel roll per child, empty spool of thread, markers or crayons, hot glue

Directions: Have the children decorate two empty toilet paper rolls each, or cut one empty paper towel roll so that each child has two rolls. Hot glue the empty spool of thread in the middle of two rolls to make a set of binoculars. Now see what you can see!

Week 2—St. Patrick's Day—Find the Gold Game

Items Needed: Juice can lids, gold spray paint, big pot or bowl

Directions: The day before, spray paint the juice can lids. Before the children arrive, hide them as if they were Easter eggs. Have the children search and find them and put them in a pot. Let the children take turns hiding the "gold" for the others.

Week 3—Big Boxes

Items Needed: Large boxes from a moving company or from the grocery store (one per child or a big one for all to share), crayons

Directions: Let the children decorate their boxes or the one big box to share. Depending on the size of the box, you may be needed to cut "windows" or "doors" in the box. Their imaginations will turn the boxes into cars, rockets, boats, trains, and houses!

Week 4—Masks from Paper Plates

Items Needed: Paper plates, crayons, Popsicle sticks, glue

Directions: Have each child draw faces on their plates, such as happy faces, sad faces, and angry faces. Attach the Popsicle sticks with glue to serve as handles. Additionally, the children can simply decorate the plates rather than create faces.

April

Week 1—Sun Catchers

Items Needed: Wax paper, crayon shavings, iron, scissors, yarn or string, hole puncher

Directions: Prepare crayon shavings ahead of time in separate piles of color and cut the wax paper into sheets about 6" X 8". Have each child sprinkle the crayon shavings onto a sheet of wax paper. Carefully put another sheet on top and lightly iron on low heat. Allow to cool for a couple of minutes, and cut into shapes, like ovals or diamonds. Punch a small hole into the top and tie the string or yarn through it. Now you can hang it!

Week 2—Shapes Mobile

Items Needed: Clothes hangers, string or yarn, various shapes such as triangles and squares drawn onto construction paper (or already cut out), safety scissors, hole puncher

Directions: Have the children cut out the shapes that were previously drawn on construction paper. (For children who are too young to cut, have the shapes pre-cut for them.) Punch a small hole in the tops of the shapes. Thread a length of string or yarn through the hole and knot. Tie the other end onto the hanger. Vary the lengths of the strings. Now you have a shapes mobile! Variations include gluing pictures cut from magazines or gluing photographs of family members onto the shapes.

Week 3—Easter/Passover—Easter Egg Hunt with Homemade Easter Baskets

Items Needed: Construction paper, yarn or ribbon, crayons, hole puncher, glue, scissors, plastic eggs filled with candy, stickers or money

Directions: Fill plastic eggs and hide them ahead of time. Give each child a sheet of construction paper on which to draw and color. Wrap the construction paper into a cone shape and glue it to hold it in place. Punch two holes on opposite sides through which you put the yarn or string. Knot both ends to make the yarn into a handle for holding the "Easter basket." Now let the children hunt for the eggs!

Week 4—Play Ball! (Or Bowling or Golf!)

Items Needed: Balls of varying sizes, six empty toilet paper rolls, empty milk cartons or small boxes, mop handle or stick

Directions: Play various activities with the balls, such as rolling the balls, throwing and catching the balls, kicking the balls. To play "bowling," set up the toilet paper rolls in the shape of a triangle as if they were pins at a bowling alley. Then "bowl" with one of the balls. In place of the toilet paper rolls, you can use plastic soda bottles, either empty or partially filled with water. Make sure the lids are on tight! You could have numbers written on the "pins" to accumulate scores if you like. To play "golf," cut the tops out of milk cartons or cut holes in small boxes. Then have the children play miniature golf by using a mop handle or stick to hit a small ball into the holes.

May

Week 1—Exploring the Backyard (or the Street or the Neighborhood)

Items Needed: Paper bags, magnifying glass (all are optional)

Directions: Give each child a bag and magnifying glass and go exploring around the backyard. Check out the different leaves, flowers, rocks, soil, sand, tree bark, grass, weeds, and even insects! How do they look, feel and smell different? Collect samples to examine later if you like.

Week 2—Relay Races and Other Running Games

Items Needed: Nothing

Directions: Races and playing tag are fun ways to burn off energy! Have each child race, or organize a relay of two or three groups of children. Vary the game from running to skipping to jumping to hopping on one foot.

All children enjoy playing tag, but this game can get out of hand! To be safe, keep it outdoors. Vary it somewhat by teaching the children how to play "Freeze Tag." In this version, the child who is "it" tries to touch the others and "freeze" them. Those who are frozen must be touched by another runner before they can resume running. Designate a safe or home base where a child can rest without worrying about being tagged.

You could also play games such as "Mother, May I?" or "1-2-3 Redlight!" For "Mother, May I?" the "Mother" picks a child and gives a command like "Take three giant steps." The child must say, "Mother, May I?" before he is allowed to follow the directions. Vary the directions. If he forgets to ask permission, he must return to the beginning. The first one to reach "Mother" takes her place.

For "1-2-3 Redlight!" the leader turns his back to the others, who are lined up, and covers his eyes. While he yells "1-2-3 Redlight," the children run to him. On "Redlight" he turns around, and the children must freeze. If the leader sees someone moving, that child returns to the beginning. The child who reaches the leader first becomes the new leader.

Week 3—T-shirt with Hand as Flower or Tree

Items Needed: White T-shirt (purchase one from a dollar store or use one you already have), fabric paint (green and brown are necessary, and other colors as desired), cardboard pieces that will fit inside the shirts

Directions: Each child gets one shirt. Put a cardboard piece in the shirt to prevent the paint from sticking both sides of the shirt together. For a boy, spread green paint onto his hand and carefully apply to the shirt. Paint a brown tree trunk to make his hand a tree. You could also dab red dots onto the "tree" to make it an apple tree. For a girl, spread any color onto her hand and carefully press her hand onto the shirt. Her hand will be a flower, so add a green stem and a leaf. Write their names on their shirts. Follow directions on the fabric paint for the amount of time to let dry.

As a Mother's Day activity and special keepsake, the moms may want to have shirts of their own with their children's handprints on them.

Week 4—Sandbox Fun

Items Needed: Sandbox, buckets, shovels

Directions: Let them play in the sand to their hearts content! Just don't let them throw it or eat it!

June

Week 1—Sidewalk Chalk

Items Needed: Sidewalk chalk

Directions: Let the children draw and write on the cement of the driveway or sidewalk. Help them practice writing their names, numbers, and the alphabet. Draw squares and use a piece of chalk for a game of "Hopscotch."

Week 2—Father's Day—Dad's Handy Little Helpers!

Items Needed: Nontoxic paint, paper suitable for painting

Directions: Each child gets one sheet of paper. Spread paint onto the palms of each hand and carefully help them put their handprints on the paper. Put their names, ages and date on the paper, and write "Dad's Handy Little Helper." It makes a wonderful Father's Day gift!

Week 3—Bubbles

Items Needed: Bubble liquid, fly swatters or bubble sticks

Directions: Have the children use fly swatters to make bubbles. It is much easier for young children to flap or swing their arms than to blow. Plus, the holes in the fly swatter make lots of little bubbles!

Week 4—Hide and Seek

Items Needed: Nothing

Directions: Start off with a parent as "it," then have the children take turns being "it." Set the boundaries for the game ahead of time so that everyone knows the area in which they are allowed to hide.

July

Week 1—Fourth of July—"Sparklers"

Items Needed: Drinking straws, colored tissue paper, tape or stapler
Directions: Cut the tissue paper into long, narrow strips about two inches wide and twelve inches long. The children can select the colors they want for their "sparkler." Tape or staple the strips of tissue to one end of the straw to make a the "sparkler." Talk about fire and fireworks safety.

Week 2—Building with Blocks

Items Needed: Lots of blocks
Directions: Help the children build houses, buildings, bridges, planes, trains, and automobiles with blocks!

Week 3—Water Sprinkler

Items Needed: Lawn sprinkler or water sprinkler toys
Directions: Let the children cool off and get out some of that energy by playing in the lawn sprinkler.

Week 4—Preschool Songs

Items Needed: Knowledge of preschool songs, such as "If You're Happy and You Know It," "Itsy Bitsy Spider," "Wheels on the Bus," "I'm a Little Teapot," "Old McDonald," "B-I-N-G-O," "Row Your Boat," "Farmer in the Dale," and "Pat-a-Cake"
Directions: Sing "movement" songs and finger play nursery rhymes. With "If You're Happy and You Know It," include various body parts, such as clap your hands, stomp your feet, pat your knees, shake your hips, wave your arms, tap your shoulders, pat your head, turn around, shout hurrah.

For "Wheels on the Bus," expand the song with wheels go round and round, wipers go swish-swish-swish, horn goes honk-honk-honk, babies go wah-wah-wah, mommies go sh-sh-sh, children go up and down.

For "Old McDonald," act out the animals on the farm as you do the sounds.

August

Week 1—Pool Fun!

Items Needed: Swimming pool or kiddie pool, children's safety floats for their arms, toy floats

Directions: Let the children play in the shallow end of the pool. Teach them to blow bubbles, duck their heads, and kick their feet. Make sure they wear children's safety floats on their arms. If none of your members have a swimming pool, use a kiddie pool.

Week 2—Modeling Clay

Items Needed: Homemade or purchased modeling clay, cookie cutters, plastic knives

Directions: Let the children make things from modeling clay. You could also help them form numbers, letters and shapes from a long clay "snake."

Week 3—"I Spy"

Items Needed: Nothing

Directions: Play "I Spy." Let a parent start off with the chant "I spy with my little eye something that is…." Select items by their colors or shapes at first until the children get used to the game. Let the children take turns "spying."

Week 4—Hand Print in Plaster

Items Needed: "Instant plaster" mix, water, Styrofoam plates, drinking straws, paint, paintbrushes, ribbon

Directions: Add necessary water to the instant plaster mix by following the directions on the label. Pour the mixture into a Styrofoam plate while you hold a drinking straw in place to serve as a hole at the top of the item. Don't overfill. Carefully press the child's hand into the mixture, pressing down as needed to make a good impression, but not all the way to the bottom. Remove the hand and allow the plaster to set according to the amount of time directed on the label. Then carefully remove hardened cast from the plate and carefully remove the straw. Thread the ribbon through this hole and tie a loop for hanging the cast. Let each child paint his or her hand.

September

Week 1—Finger Paint Masterpieces

Items Needed: Nontoxic finger paint, paper, sponges cut into various shapes

Directions: Children should wear smocks to cover their clothes. For one picture, wet the paper first before they finger paint. For another picture, leave the paper dry to get a different effect. Talk about the different colors you get when you mix colors. Let them use the sponges to design their pictures.

Week 2—"Duck, Duck, Goose," "Ring Around the Rosy," Musical Chairs, and Leap Frog

Items Needed: Chairs or rugs/mats or carpet remnants

Directions: For "Duck, Duck, Goose," have children sit in a circle. The "goose" walks around the circle tapping each "duck" on the head. On one of them, he says "Goose," and that child chases him around the circle. If he is caught before sitting in the empty spot, he is the "goose" again. If he makes it safely to the empty spot, the other child becomes the "goose."

For "Ring Around the Rosy," everyone forms a circle holding hands. Go around and around chanting: "Ring around the rosy/Pocket full of posies/Ashes, ashes.../We all fall down!" Then collapse on the floor when you sing "all fall down!"

For Musical Chairs, you can use chairs or small rugs or mats on the floor. Small children may find the mats easier. Start the game off with one mat per child. Let the children know that when you stop the music, they should sit on a mat. Then take away one mat and begin the music. When you stop the music again, one child will be "out" because she couldn't get to a mat. Take away another one and begin again.

Week 3—Collages

Items Needed: Construction paper, glue, scissors, various magazines or pictures already cut out featuring children, houses, cars, trucks, trees, flowers, suns, etc.

Directions: Have each child create collages of varying themes using the pictures found in magazines. Some themes include the "Alphabet" featuring a picture for each letter, or "Numbers," "Toys, "My House," "My Family."

Week 4—Flashlight Pounce

Items Needed: At least one flashlight, preferably one for every three children

Directions: Shine the flashlight around on the floor and have the children try to catch or jump on the beam! This works best with about three children per flashlight. Then, have them take turns using the flashlight.

October

Week 1—Leaf Collage

Items Needed: Construction paper, glue, leaves

Directions: Take the children for a nature walk to collect leaves. Once back inside, glue the leaves to a sheet of construction paper to form a leafy collage.

Week 2—"Do the Hokey Pokey"

Items Needed: Nothing

Directions: Gather in a circle, and do the "Hokey Pokey!" The words are: "Put your right arm in, put your right arm out, put your right arm in and you shake it all about. You do the Hokey Pokey and you turn yourself around. That's what it's all about!" Do all parts of the body: right and left shoulders, elbows, hands, arms, knees, feet, legs, plus the head, bottom and tummy.

Week 3—Bake Cookies

Items Needed: Pre-packaged cookie dough from the refrigerated section of your local grocery store, cookie cutters, sprinkles, flour, wax paper, cookie sheet

Directions: Follow directions on the package of the cookie dough. Allow the children to cut out shapes and decorate the cookies. Afterwards, eat the cookies for snack!

Week 4—Halloween—"Pin the Mouth on the Pumpkin"

Items Needed: Drawing of a pumpkin cut from a large orange poster board, eyes and nose of jack-o-lantern cut from black construction paper and glued to the "pumpkin," jack-o-lantern mouths cut from black construction paper with each child's name on them, tape, blindfold

Directions: Take turns blindfolding the children and allowing them to "Pin the Mouth on the Pumpkin," but use tape instead of a pin.

November

Week 1—Lifesize Drawing

Items Needed: Crayons, "end roll" from your local newspaper ("End rolls" are usually given away free; you just have to call the newspaper office and ask for them.)

Directions: Spread out the end roll from a newspaper and have the child lie on it. Trace around his body and clothes. Once he colors it, the picture is a lifesize portrait!

Week 2—Play Games

Items Needed: Favorite children's games
Directions: Have each child bring his or her favorite game to playgroup. Some suitable games may include "Candyland," "Chutes and Ladders," "Hi-Ho Cherrio," "Memory," "Trouble," "UNO," "Old Maid," "Go Fish," and "Twister."

Week 3—Thanksgiving—Color a Turkey Hand

Items Needed: Drawing paper, crayons
Directions: Position each child's hand on the paper so that the fingers are spread apart and trace it. The thumb becomes the turkey's head, and the fingers are the tail feathers. Draw legs and let the children color their turkey.

Week 4—Tumbling/Gymnastics

Items Needed: Large open area with carpeting or mats
Directions: Have the children take turns tumbling. Children enjoy doing forward rolls, log rolls, "egg rolls," and practicing cartwheels and backbends. Remember to do warm-up exercises first just to stretch their arm and leg muscles.

December

Week 1—Paper Christmas Tree

Items Needed: Green construction paper cut in a large triangle, "ornaments" cut out of various colors of construction paper, glue, glitter
Directions: Have the children decorate their own paper Christmas trees.

Week 2—Reindeer Hands & Feet

Items needed: Black and brown construction paper, scissors, pencil, markers or crayons, glue

Directions: From the brown construction paper, trace one foot and cut it out. From the black construction paper, trace and cut out both hands with fingers spread apart. Glue the hands to the top of the foot where the toes are to make the "antlers" of the reindeer. The foot is its face, with the heel being the nose. Now your child can draw the features of the face, or you can have pre-cut eyes, noses, and mouths for him to glue onto the face.

Week 3—Santa Face

Items Needed: White construction paper, red construction paper, crayons, white cotton balls, glue

Directions: Cut the white construction paper into a circle for the face and a triangle for the beard. Cut the red construction paper into a triangle for the hat. Glue them together. Have your child fill up the beard by gluing on the cotton balls, make a band of cotton balls around the hat, and use one cotton ball at the tip of the hat. Draw in the eyes, nose and mouth.

Week 4—Christmas/Hanukkah—Sing Holiday Songs

Items Needed: CDs or cassette tapes of holiday songs, or just knowledge of holiday songs

Directions: Before, after, or instead of exchanging gifts, sing holiday songs. Children particularly love "Jingle Bells," "Santa Claus Is Coming to Town," "Frosty the Snowman," and "Rudolf the Red-Nosed Reindeer."

Extra Weeks

Week 1—Walk Around the Block

Items Needed: Tricycles, big wheels, wagons, strollers (all are optional)
Directions: Take your tykes for a stroll around the block or the park!
You'll all benefit from the fresh air and exercise.

Week 2—Tent

Items Needed: Large sheets and blankets, tables and chairs
Directions: Drape large sheets and blankets over combinations of
tables and chairs to form a tent or a fort or a castle or whatever their
imaginations make it!

Week 3—Family Book

Items Needed: Several sheets of paper (plain white or construction paper), glue, scissors, yarn, hole puncher, crayons, pictures of
family members
Directions: Help your child put together a "book" with pictures of
family members and drawings made by the child about the family.
Afterwards, stack the pages, hole punch two or three holes along the left
side, and string yarn through the holes to hold the "book" together.

Week 4—Build a Snowman

Items Needed: Snow, items to use for eyes, nose and mouth (buttons,
pebbles, raisins, etc.), sticks for arms, miscellaneous clothing such as
scarves, hats, mittens, etc.
Directions: Bundle the children and take them out in the snow to
build a snowman or snowwoman! Plan on making a fairly small snowman, so that it will be finished before the children grow bored. Make

snow angels and enjoy a good old-fashioned snowball fight before you head back inside!

CHAPTER 10

LEADING YOUR PLAYGROUP
SUCCESSFULLY

Once the initial legwork of starting a playgroup is over, the amount of management a playgroup requires depends mainly on the size of the group. The more members there are, the more work it will take to manage it, unless you delegate the duties. Generally, however, moms and children prefer a small number of members anyway, because a small group is easier to supervise and is more intimate and spontaneous than a larger group. However, whether providing a structured activity or free play for the children, even a small playgroup needs some management by a recognized leader.

To make it easier for you, here are some tips a leader can use to manage a playgroup effectively and keep it successful.

Structure of the Playgroup

Most of the time a playgroup leader is the one who initially started the playgroup, so the group has been designed specifically to meet her needs and those of her children. She made the preliminary decisions about such issues as how often the playgroup should meet, whether children will participate in structured activities or just free play, and what discipline policies should be in place.

However, to make the playgroup successful and one that others would want to join, other members' desires must be considered as well. Actually, most playgroups would benefit from instituting a few basic guidelines or rules from the very first meeting, rather than try to introduce them later. If possible, have a few guidelines written down, and pass out copies for the members at the very first meeting. Any changes can be made that day, or you can suggest they look over the list and consider modifications or additions at the next playgroup session.

You may also want to have a few additional copies of the guidelines on hand at every meeting for visitors to the playgroup and for new members later on.

Some leaders want to maintain primary control of their playgroups, while others feel more comfortable delegating some of the responsibilities. Both methods are effective; it's up to you. The method you choose may also depend on what other activities you are involved in, how much extra time you have, how interested the other members may be in volunteering to help, and how large the playgroup is.

If the playgroup is large enough, it may benefit to have officers to help. You don't want to burn out from doing too much. The following is a list of officers for a large mothers' group. Your playgroup may need all or just one or two officers depending on the activities of the group. These officers are in addition to the playgroup leader or president.

1. The Vice President assists the President.

2. The Secretary keeps up with participation and enrollment, takes the minutes of business meetings, and prepares copies of the minutes for distribution.

3. The Treasurer manages all finances of the organization.

4. The Membership Coordinator works closely with the Treasurer to keep track of the status of each member, then compiles, prints and distributes a membership roster.

5. The Librarian maintains the collection of parenting books and videos.

6. The Newsletter Editor collects information, designs, prints and distributes a monthly newsletter.

7. The Webmaster designs and maintains the web site.

8. The Babysitting Co-op/Playgroup Coordinator supervises the services of the co-op and the various playgroups.

9. The Social Activities Coordinator organizes family functions and field trips.

10. The Outreach Coordinator handles publicity for the group to attract new members and organizes community service projects.

A small playgroup of ten or less will not entail nearly so many responsibilities! As a result, the leader usually carries out any necessary duties, or members volunteer as the need arises. Actually, the most important responsibility for a leader is to attend playgroup faithfully and keep the ball rolling.

Usually the person who initiates the playgroup serves as the leader or coordinator until she moves away or until her children start school. At that time, she can pass the baton to another mom who feels as strongly about the playgroup as she does, or the playgroup can elect another leader. A few playgroups, such as those on military bases, elect new leaders every year.

Current Members

Managing a playgroup entails very little maintenance. You may need to call or email moms to remind them about the group, or your guidelines may require the hostess to call the members each week. However, the day after playgroup, the leader should call the moms who were absent. This courtesy call lets them know they were missed, gives them a chance to ask for help for a personal need if necessary, and provides them an opportunity to express any problems with playgroup. While you're on the phone, let them know where playgroup will be next week.

Occasionally, conflicts may occur between members of playgroup. A leader may feel comfortable mediating between the two moms, or she may prefer to let the two work it out themselves. However, if some of the members of playgroup have a complaint against another mom or her child, it is the responsibility of the leader to handle the situation. Sometimes talking to the mom will clear up any misunderstandings, or perhaps the leader can suggest a new rule for the group that will clear up the matter and avert further problems. For example, if one little boy is repeatedly hurting the other children, the leader can talk to the mother about watching her child more closely, or she can suggest that the children play in the same area with the parents so all the children will be supervised more closely.

To keep current members actively involved and informed, you may want to establish additional services and benefits. Read the chapter "Including Parents in on the Fun" for details on how to do them. Not all of these will be appropriate or feasible for your playgroup, but you may want to consider instituting:

- A monthly or quarterly newsletter
- A monthly calendar
- A web site
- Email reminders

Use the Internet whenever possible as an efficient means of managing your playgroup. Web sites such as OnlinePlaygroup.com, PlaydateConnection.com and Slowlane.com offer various resources you can use to make things easier.

New Members

In a small playgroup, the leader usually decides when the group has gotten too small and initiates the plan to "recruit" new members. This may occur anywhere from eighteen months to two years after starting the playgroup, when families move, children start school, or moms go back to work fulltime. Playgroups have a fairly high turnover rate, so regularly reviewing the number of active participants and adding new members when needed is a good idea.

It's very easy to "recruit" new members because it's basically the same method you probably used to start your playgroup. Just follow the detailed methods listed in the chapter "Step-by-Step Guide to Starting Your Playgroup." Basically, all you need to do is:

- Post flyers in local libraries and area businesses frequented by parents.
- Check playgroup directories on the Internet for those who may be seeking playgroups.
- Advertise in your local newspaper.
- Send photo releases to local newspapers.
- Distribute flyers in other neighborhoods.
- Spread the word to everyone you meet.

You may choose one procedure, or combine several for maximum benefit. Additionally, if you continually update the flyers around your community and publicize your playgroup's activities through periodic press releases, you may never have to recruit at all.

When a potential member calls for more information about the playgroup, be prepared to give information about the number of moms in the group, the number and ages of the children, and other general information regarding when and where you meet. Invite her to visit playgroup at the next session, and give her directions to the location. Be sure to get her name, her children's names and her phone number. Don't forget to notify the playgroup hostess to expect extra guests.

If playgroup will not be at your house that week, consider offering to meet the new mom at a public place first and having her follow you to the location. That way, she will get a chance to meet someone ahead of time and won't feel so nervous about attending a function for the first time among strangers. She also won't have to worry about following directions and finding the location, which may be difficult for someone in a new and unfamiliar city.

When people are visiting playgroup for the first time, treat them with the courtesy you would extend to any guest in your home. Greet them at the door and introduce them to the other parents and children. Try to include them in the conversations. Get to know them by asking a few questions, but don't be too nosy! Try to coax their children into joining the play, but don't push too hard. Children will usually cling to mom the first couple of visits to playgroup anyway.

Even if playgroup is not held at your house that week, try to make visitors feel as comfortable in the group as possible. Most likely you were their first contact with the playgroup, so they will look to you for introductions and information as if you were the hostess. If the hostess does not greet visitors at the door, you welcome them to playgroup and introduce them to everyone. After all, as the leader you are the spokesperson for the group.

Give the visitors copies of the playgroup roster and guidelines. The guidelines should answer any questions they may have, especially any questions that they may find awkward to ask in a group setting.

The day after playgroup, call each visitor and tell her how much the group enjoyed meeting her and her children. Give her an opportunity to ask any follow-up questions she may have. Invite her to return next week and give directions to the location.

After two visits to playgroup, you may suggest that she join playgroup. By this time, she should know if your playgroup will provide what she and her children need. Ask her if she would like to be put on the playgroup list, but don't be offended if she doesn't want to join the playgroup. She may be looking for something else for herself and her children. If you know of other playgroups in the area, suggest that she try one of those.

Once a new mom has joined playgroup, update the playgroup phone list for everyone.

Let the new mom attend playgroup several times before she has to host it. Perhaps go through one entire rotation or give her at least five visits before she has to take her turn. Inform her of the duties of a hostess so she can prepare.

If you and one or two of the other members get together outside of playgroup, consider inviting the new mom to join you. Being included in impromptu playdates will make her feel part of the group and will give her and all of you a chance to get to know each other better.

Rotation

It is up to the playgroup leader to keep up with rotation, although each member should have some idea of when it will be her turn to host. Whether playgroup is hosted on a volunteer basis or on a rotation based on the phone list, someone needs to know where the group is in the rotation. The leader can simply make vocal reminders during playgroup about who is next to host and who comes after her, etc. Other leaders prefer to print a calendar each month. A printed calendar makes a handy reference, but only if members do not switch too often. If your playgroup members switch frequently, your calendar will be useless and more confusing than helpful. Also, you may have to print revised calendars so often that it would be cheaper and more convenient to announce the upcoming hosts during playgroup.

Occasionally, the next person scheduled to host will not be at playgroup the week before so that you can remind her. In this case, during your follow-up call, remind her that her turn is coming up and confirm that she will be able to take it. Sometimes this may feel awkward. Some playgroup leaders want to avoid the feeling that they are "nagging," so they ask someone else in playgroup to check with her. This is perfectly acceptable, especially if she spends a lot of time with another mom in playgroup and they have become good friends.

If a mom cannot host playgroup during her week, she can arrange to switch with another mom, or she may feel more comfortable calling the leader. If so, the leader then needs to make other arrangements for playgroup. Sometimes this may be a last minute situation, but it shouldn't be too difficult to arrange an alternative location. A few options may be available besides canceling playgroup altogether. You could offer to host the group in your home or you could call another mom who may be able to do it. Keep in mind that hosting playgroup generally requires cleaning house and buying snacks, so some moms may not be prepared to host playgroup at the last minute. They would need a day or two to prepare. Another option would be to have playgroup at the park or some other location. Wherever the new location will be, call all the members to let them know.

If your group already meets in a central location, your responsibilities may vary. Generally, you should try to arrive early to ensure that the rooms you need are ready, and you may need to be one of the last to leave to ensure that everything has been returned to its proper place. Of course, delegate such duties as bringing snacks and cleaning up. The same few members should not have to do all the work, so you may want to rotate the duties.

Even in a large facility, your group needs to establish guidelines and rules, particularly regarding the supervision and behavior of the children. Supervision may rotate among the parents or you may want to hire a babysitter, but keep in mind that an adult should ultimately be in charge.

After the first session in the facility, send a thank you card. You need to maintain a good relationship with the owners of the facility, particularly if they allow you to use it free of charge. Even if you are renting, you should let them know how much your group appreciates their generosity.

Your appreciation should extend to any field trip hosts and special speakers as well. The playgroup leader or the person who organizes the field trips should send thank you notes on behalf of the group.

General Management Tips

Although managing a playgroup is not the same as managing a business, you may benefit by adapting a few business management tips to your playgroup situation. Use these tips to get the most out of your group:

- Lead by example. Don't expect your members to arrive on time if you are consistently late. They won't pick up toys after their children if you don't pick up after yours. Examples of this can go on and on.

- Prioritize and delegate. As a parent, there are a lot of demands on your time, but your time and energy are limited. Focus your energies on what is important to you, do that first, and delegate the rest. It is better to do a few things and do them well than to do a lot of things, but none of them well.

- Fan the flames of enthusiasm. When people first join your group they will be all fired up and ready to do great things. Get them involved while they are most enthusiastic and eager.

- Seek input from the group, and listen to it. You may be surprised at what you can learn.

- Relax and enjoy yourself! Playgroup is supposed to be a fun time for you and your child.

CHAPTER 11

OVERCOMING PROBLEMS YOU MAY ENCOUNTER

A s with any organization, you may encounter a few obstacles in starting your playgroup and a few snags in maintaining your group, but generally they may be overcome with a little preparation and a little deft handling. What you are doing is worthwhile, so don't let anything stand in the way of starting and enjoying your playgroup!

Here are some problems you may encounter along the way and various solutions with which to overcome them.

Unruly Children

If your playgroup is a manageable size, but the children often tend to get out of hand, try one of the following suggestions to alleviate the problem:

- Reduce playgroup time from two hours to an hour and a half. Depending on the ages of the children, they may be getting cranky because they are getting tired.

- Engage the children in various planned activities rather than an exclusive playtime. This way the parents can keep them occupied and entertained in a more structured environment.

- If you already combine both crafts and some free playtime, switch the order in which they are done. Start with free play to release their pent up energy before leading them into the craft or activity. If you can't calm them down for the craft, start with the craft and end with free play instead.

- Ensure direct adult supervision of the children. Some playgroups establish a rule early on that the moms and children remain in the same play area so that the moms can supervise and prevent accidents and conflicts. If one area for everyone is not feasible, simply take turns supervising the children. Depending on how many parents are in playgroup and how long the playgroup sessions last, each mom would need to spend only about ten or fifteen minutes in direct supervision of the children.

- Find a larger location. Host playgroup in your backyard or meet at the park.

- Bring out a short children's video to calm things down. However, since child-to-child interaction is low during movies, just be careful to limit the movie time as much as possible.

- Add a snack break. If you don't have one, a snack can effectively divide the playtime and give the children the break they may need to calm down for a while before resuming their play.

- Move the snack break to earlier or later if you already serve snacks.

- Serve healthy snacks rather than sweets.

Childcare Supervisors

Supervision of the children is a prime consideration in playgroup. Your children must be able to interact and play in a safe environment. If the group is small, every parent should be responsible for watching her own child throughout the playgroup session. If the children are separated from the parents, or if they generally play in an adjoining playroom, each parent can take turns supervising the children. Some large mothers' groups provide childcare through volunteers. Ask your church for possible suggestions. Some large groups hire babysitters, either adults or homeschooled teenagers, and pay them through membership dues or donations.

Clingy Child

Many children feel shy when encountering new people. Reassure each mom that, almost without exception, all children initially will cling to mom and seem overwhelmed by the others at first. Be prepared for some to be a little more shy and reserved than others. They may prefer to stay near their moms and watch for a while. Don't worry; they just need some time to check things out. Give them the time they need without pushing. They will warm up to the group and join right in after a few weeks.

Problem Child

Every playgroup will have a "wild child" at one time or another. Usually a boy between the ages of two and three-and-a-half, this child is active, energetic, loud, and into everything. He often plays rough, may not like to share, and will aggressively defend his toys and territory. Don't overreact to his negative behavior. Just keep an eye on him so he won't hurt the other children and then wait out this phase. Usually before he turns four, he will have calmed down considerably. If his mother will watch him to prevent accidents from happening and to reprimand him as needed, the other moms will not develop resentment toward the child and his mom. Also, keeping the play area in the same room with the moms will go a long way to preventing problems with this "wild child."

Now, a "wild child" is not necessarily the same as a child who causes serious problems, and the group should agree on acceptable and unacceptable standards of behavior. For example, a child who bites should not be tolerated. Speak to the parent of the child who displays serious anti-social behavior such as biting, and if the problem is not resolved, do not hesitate to ask the parent and child to leave playgroup for a while.

Siblings or a Wide Age Range

The problem with playgroups designed specifically for a certain age group or particular type of child is what to do about siblings. Unless your playgroup meets in the evenings or on weekends where other family members can stay home with the other children, the siblings will have to be included in the playgroup. However, the degree to which they are included is up to the group. If the playgroup ranges in age from newborn to kindergarten, then you shouldn't have any problems. Most likely the age range will prohibit structured activities anyway, and the group will participate in free play. The only time older siblings may pose a problem is during the summer when school-aged children will be home and will expand the size of the playgroup. Then your playgroup needs to decide if it will take a break for the summer, find a larger facility in which to meet, or try to accommodate the older kids as best they can. Remember, warmer weather means playgroup can meet in the backyard or at the park where a large group can spread out.

If playgroup includes a wide range of ages, try to keep the babies who are on the floor in a safe area of the room where older children won't accidentally bother them. Maybe put them on a blanket with their toys and tell the other children that area is off limits.

Don't worry about not having infant toys. Generally, babies enjoy watching older kids play. At the same time, don't worry if you don't have any toys for children over one year of age. Children will find new ways of playing with any kind of toy, even one designed for infants. You can always resolve the problem by having everyone take a few toys to play with at your house.

Getting to Know Each Other

You may hesitate to join a playgroup or start one because you're nervous among strangers. *What will we find to talk about at the first gathering?* Set your mind at ease. You already have something in common with all those strangers: your children. Discuss what they've recently learned how to do, a cute thing they did or said, or any problem you may be having. You'll soon find that the group feels like a gathering of longtime friends rather than a group of strangers who just met! Occasionally there will be moments of awkward silences, particularly if the group is small, but they will pass or the children will fill them. If all else fails, fall back on the old standbys for all moms: Discuss labor and delivery, how each of you met and married your husbands, or where you all grew up. As you get to know each other, the silences will be fewer and further between.

Besides, at the first meeting, you'll have several decisions the group will need to make. You may want to discuss such issues as how often the playgroup should meet, whether or not a small membership fee should be charged, and what discipline policies should be in place. Give everyone a chance to meet each other and socialize first, then bring up these issues when playgroup is about half over. Discussing the guidelines for the group should fill the remaining time of the first meeting. Once that first meeting is over, the subsequent gatherings will get more and more comfortable as you grow to know each other.

However, no matter how comfortable the group members seem to be with each other over time, there are two topics of conversation that the rules of etiquette say you should avoid. Never discuss politics or religion. Both are very personal decisions about which people feel very strongly. Except in a Bible study group, or a similar religious or political group, you would do well to follow this advice!

Late Arrivals

After the first few playgroup sessions, you may find that nearly everyone arrives between fifteen and thirty minutes after the official start of playgroup. This is normal, as the members are growing comfortable with the group. Besides, we all know how difficult it sometimes is to arrive anywhere on time with children in tow! If latecomers are causing problems, consider changing the starting time for playgroup. Otherwise, just tactfully remind them of the playgroup's time schedule; this reminder may have to be done on a regular basis every few months or so.

If the adults or children engage in planned activities, do not feel that you have to delay until everyone arrives. That is not fair to those who were on time. Besides, if latecomers realize they will miss part of the activities, it may serve as an incentive to arrive on time.

Lingerers

Those who arrive late may linger late as well. As a matter of fact, even those who arrived on time may linger past the official end of playgroup, especially if they are having a good time. Consider it a compliment. Your playgroup is a success! They are enjoying themselves so much that they don't want to leave! However, if members consistently linger week after week, perhaps your playgroup is not long enough. Consider extending it to two hours. On the other hand, if playgroup must end by a certain time, take the initiative by starting to pick up toys or helping to clean up about fifteen minutes before playgroup officially should end. The other members should take the hint and respond accordingly. Also, it would not be rude for you to remind the membership in a tactful way that playgroup needs to end by a certain time.

Complaint Sessions

One pitfall to avoid is allowing playgroup to become a complaint session, where moms spend most of their time whining about their husbands or children. Certainly, moms should be free to express their problems and discontent, and you should acknowledge their complaints. However, playgroup should be a supportive and uplifting time for everyone. If the discussion begins to deteriorate into a gripe session, steer the conversation to other topics.

Personality Conflicts

After the group has grown to know each other, most everyone will get along. Occasionally, as with any group dynamic, there are bound to be some causes for friction and even personality conflicts now and then. The most common occur between children. However, if you and the other moms focus on the children and their interactions with each other during the playgroup sessions, you should be able to avert potential problems before they occur. Try not to overreact to your child or another child's negative behavior because conflicts are likely to occur from time to time.

Misunderstandings resulting from their children's behavior may occasionally cause friction among members. Usually, these situations can be cleared up easily by communication between the two moms and by keeping a close watch on the children to prevent potential problems. Also, make it clear that each mother must be allowed to discipline her own children in her own manner.

Occasionally, conflicts may occur between members of playgroup. Some leaders may feel comfortable mediating between the two moms, or they may prefer to let the two work it out themselves. However, if most of the members of playgroup have a complaint against another mom or her child, it is the responsibility of the leader to handle the situation. Sometimes talking to the mom will clear up any misunderstandings, or perhaps the leader can suggest a new rule for the group that will clear up the matter and avert further problems.

Another situation that may cause discord is if two moms tend to emerge as leaders. One may not want to be a follower and may even resist compromise. The best thing to do is to put every decision to a vote by the whole group. If everyone votes on decisions, no one can be labeled as a dictator, just as no one can claim that her viewpoints were not considered. If someone has a different vision for the group than what the others want, that mom should start her own group.

Remember, your playgroup may not be right for all mothers and children who visit. Not every visitor will want to participate regularly. Try not to take it personally when a mom quits. Honestly, it is better that she seek another playgroup that suits her needs rather than stay with your group and possibly cause problems. Also, don't hesitate to ask someone to leave playgroup if they or their children are causing problems.

Low Attendance

If you have just started your playgroup and you are experiencing low attendance, this is normal. Expect the greatest number to attend the first session, and then drop off for a few sessions. There may actually be a time or two when only one mom shows up! This has happened with the Millbrook Area Playgroup a handful of times. Don't get discouraged and don't give up. Those absent members may have had prior commitments they couldn't change, or they could have forgotten about playgroup entirely. It will take a few weeks for playgroup to become a habit.

Keep in mind that no matter how many total members you have, the number of consistent active participants will be lower. Not everyone will be able to attend every session. Someone may be sick; someone may have a prior commitment; someone else may have family visiting. For example, Millbrook Area Playgroup usually maintains about ten members, but only about six to eight moms attend regularly. Occasionally, we'll have a playgroup session with every member present, but this seldom happens. We deal with a big playgroup one week, so that we can still have an adequate number the other weeks.

There are various ways to help alleviate an attendance problem in the beginning and later on. Here are a few suggestions:

- Make sure the day and time for playgroup is convenient for the majority of members. If another day and time would be better, change it and see if that makes a difference. For two years, the Millbrook Area Playgroup met every Wednesday morning. One summer, we changed it to Friday mornings to accommodate one mom who began a part-time summer job, and we changed it back again in the fall when her job ended.

- Do your best to stick to the agreed day and time. You may be inclined to want to be as flexible as possible so that everyone will be able to attend each week. Unfortunately, a successful playgroup cannot be that flexible from week to week. A variable meeting schedule can cause confusion, and the playgroup's momentum will be lost.

- Call members a day or two before playgroup to remind them about it, or send them email reminders. Forgetting about playgroup is the number one reason for missing it, next to an illness in the family, according to many playgroup participants. Reminders are important!

- Print a monthly or quarterly calendar.

- Consider publishing a monthly or quarterly newsletter with a calendar of events.

- Add a notice in your newsletter or email every few months stating that if a member does not notify you that they want to remain part of the group, they will be eliminated from the communications list. This will get a few problem members off the list.

- Consider having a web site with a calendar of events.

- Call or email those members who were absent from playgroup within a couple of days to let them know they were missed and to find out if they are still interested in playgroup.

- Get others involved by soliciting ideas for playdates and special activities, especially if you don't always meet in your homes. If members have input regarding activities, they may be more inclined to participate. Also, you will be able to weed out those members who are not pulling their weight if they must participate in playgroup in order to attend special activities.

- Establish additional services and benefits such as those described in "Including Parents in on the Fun," and get your other members involved by delegating those tasks to them.

- Devise rosters for such duties as cleaning and crafts. Even ordinary tasks can make members feel needed.

- Establish officers to involve others in the organization.
- Consider charging membership dues. Usually, if people have to pay for something, they are more likely to use it. Fitness clubs use that as an incentive all the time.
- Consider instituting other requirements, in addition to or in place of dues. For example, the only requirement for membership in the Millbrook Area Playgroup is for each mom to take her turn hosting playgroup in her home. Usually, if a mom has to go to the trouble of hosting playgroup when it's her turn in rotation, she will make an effort to attend the other playgroup sessions, or she will definitely terminate her membership.
- Review your membership periodically to see if you need to add new members. Morale will suffer if your group claims a membership of thirty, but only five show up for activities. Rather than low attendance, you may actually be experiencing low membership.

Low Membership

Periodically, you should review the number of active participants and consider adding new members if needed. Over time, you will have a number of moms join and quit for various reasons; families move, children start school, moms go back to work, or an only child doesn't get along in a group setting. Many times two children and their moms will hit it off, and they will get together so much outside of playgroup that they really don't need playgroup anymore. If a military base is located nearby, you may find your playgroup in transition even more frequently as military families come and go. In some areas of the country, the high cost of living requires a two-income family, so there will be very few stay-at-home moms. For whatever reasons, your playgroup may drop to an inadequately small number of members from time to time. On average, this happens to the Millbrook Area Playgroup about every eighteen months to two years.

When it happens, don't get discouraged and don't panic. Simply "recruit" more moms. Remember the procedures you used to start the playgroup? Follow them for increasing the playgroup, or read the chapter "Step-by-Step Guide to Starting Your Playgroup." Periodically, you and the other moms may need to:

- Post flyers in local libraries, churches and area businesses frequented by parents. In some business locations, leaflets may work better than posters. Sometimes people will take leaflets but they won't copy down a phone number from a poster. Additionally, if you keep the flyers in your community up-to-date, you may never need to "recruit" at all.

- Check Internet playgroup directories, such as OnlinePlaygroup.com and PlaydateConnection.com, for those who may be seeking playgroups and add your group to their lists.

- Advertise in your local newspaper.

- Send photo releases to local newspapers.

- Distribute flyers in area neighborhoods. If you don't receive an adequate response, widen your target area to include other neighborhoods and try again. Continue this process until you have reached the number of members you want.

- Spread the word to everyone you meet.

- Consider designing business cards for your members, so they will have something to give out to people who seem interested in playgroup. There are several kits on the market for printing business cards at home, and they are fairly inexpensive and very simple to use. Otherwise, give each member a few flyers to hand out when needed.

Too Many Members

If you keep the flyers in area businesses up-to-date or if you live in an area with a large percentage of at-home moms, you may experience the opposite of dwindling membership—too many members. What a wonderful problem to have! Generally, groups of ten moms or less can meet in each other's homes comfortably. Although apartments and military base housing are usually small, even they have a living room where the parents can congregate and a bedroom where the children can play.

If your group exceeds ten moms, you now have two solutions from which to choose. First, the playgroup can split into two or more groups in order to continue meeting in each other's homes. These smaller groups may be divided according to region or to the ages of the children. Keep in mind that a mom may have children who would belong to two different groups; she can either participate in both or pick the one she prefers. Every once in a while, get all the groups together a trip to the zoo or a special party.

The second solution is to find a suitable meeting space for the entire playgroup in a church or community center. To prevent the playgroup sessions from becoming out of control in such a large group, definitely set up guidelines and rules.

Location

Sometimes problems arise regarding the location of playgroup. If one location doesn't work for your group, try to find a better place to meet. Here are some suggestions:

- "Share" playgroup with another mom if your home is too small. In this case, one mom hosts playgroup in her home while the other provides the snacks. To ensure that all goes well, the one bringing snacks should consider what the other mom usually serves, make sure she brings enough for everyone who may attend, and stay to help clean up afterwards.

- Gather the group in the backyard where the children can spread out and be as loud as they want!

- See if you can meet at a local church, library, community center, neighborhood clubhouse, or YMCA. Ask input from your members; perhaps one may be a member of a church that will have space for your group.

- Divide the group into two smaller groups based on age or region.

- Meet at a local park or playground. They are usually large enough to accommodate groups of any size. However, winter weather may prohibit use of an outdoor location.

- Visit area attractions for playgroup. In this case, take the children to the beach, lake, zoo and mall. Visit amusement parks, water parks, museums, arcades and fast-food restaurants with play areas. Depending on the children's ages, you could also take them bowling, roller skating and swimming for an interesting change. See what attractions your hometown has to offer.

Rotation

You may find some members hesitant about taking their turn to host playgroup. They may not want the group in their home for various reasons; maybe they feel their home is too small, they don't have toys for the older or younger children, they may be on a tight financial budget, or they have valuable artwork or antiques. Sometimes they just don't like the hassle! However, it is not fair to those who do take their turn for others to get out of it. If your group is hosted on a volunteer basis, the leader should tactfully remind those members that they haven't hosted in a while. An easy remedy would be to follow an alphabetical phone list for rotation.

If someone is still reluctant to host playgroup in her home, she can "share" playgroup with another mom. In this case, one mom hosts playgroup in her home while the other provides the snacks. Or playgroup could meet at a central location that week, and the hostess could provide the snacks.

Occasionally, the next person scheduled to host will not be at playgroup the week before her turn. In this case, during your follow-up call, remind her that her turn is coming up and confirm that she will be able to take it. Sometimes this may feel awkward. Some playgroup leaders want to avoid the feeling that they are "nagging," so they ask someone else in playgroup to check with her. This is perfectly acceptable, especially if she spends a lot of time with another mom in playgroup and they have become good friends. However, you should make it clear to all members that missing playgroup does not mean they can get out of their turn to host, or you may have lots of members missing playgroup the week before their turn in an attempt to be skipped in the rotation!

Of course, there are legitimate reasons why you should skip certain members during rotation. Some moms who may be skipped completely during one or two rotations include new moms to the group, those who are in the last month of pregnancy, moms who have newborn infants, or moms whose families have just had the flu or other contagious illness.

Cleaning Up

It is amazing how some adults will try to get out of cleaning up just as regularly as most children will! In a playgroup in your home, there may be one or two moms who will gather her children and belongings and leave without helping to clean up or even asking her children to pick up toys. Even in a central location such as a community center, you will probably find that the same few members week after week are staying to clean up after others have left. This isn't fair, and it is likely to cause resentment eventually.

Here are some ideas that may alleviate the problem:

- Make sure you do your share when playgroup meets at other houses! The hostesses will appreciate it, and they may be more likely to return the favor later.

- Start cleaning up about fifteen minutes before the end of playgroup or before the first parent usually leaves.

- Direct your children to pick up toys in a voice loud enough for other parents to hear, but not too obviously loud. Perhaps announce to all the children to follow you so that you can all pick up toys before playgroup ends.

- Delegate tasks, such as asking one mom if she would mind picking up the blocks real quick or asking another mom to collect the scattered plates and napkins for you while you're cleaning off the counter.

- Rotate cleaning duties among the members if you meet in a central facility. Divide everyone into two or three smaller groups based on last names, or rotate two at a time. Make it part of your guidelines.

Communication

Sometimes communication among members may suffer in a playgroup, especially if your group is very large or if you live far apart from each other in a large city or in neighboring towns. To keep members informed and connected, you may want to institute a newsletter or calendar that can be mailed or emailed to members. Both may serve as excellent reminders for upcoming events and activities. A newsletter doesn't have to be elaborate. To start, simply include a list of your members, calendar of special events, schedule of playgroup locations, and descriptions of what happened at recent events. Later you could add favorite recipes, reviews of children's books or movies or toys, and rainy day activities for children. Encourage parents and children to submit items, such as articles or poems or pictures.

For families online, a web site can serve as an e-newsletter and a central location for your group to list members, plan activities and post calendars. Remember, do not refer to last names, addresses or phone numbers on your web site, and check with members first before posting photographs of the children.

A web site is not the only way to reach your members over the Internet. Many individuals now have email addresses and go online frequently. Keep in contact with your members through email. With email, they can respond when it's convenient for them, and you can eliminate any long distance phone charges that may apply. Email your members to remind them about upcoming events, to reschedule playdates, and to follow up on any missed playgroup sessions. It's often quicker and easier than picking up the phone! Just get their email addresses when you get their other information, make sure it all remains confidential, and remind everyone to check their email regularly or at least the day before an event to find out if any changes have been made.

A phone tree may be essential for a large group. With a phone tree, information gets disseminated to every member quickly and easily.

Each member has only three or four other members to have to call, then those three or four have three or four others, and so on.

For a large mothers' group, consider forming care groups. These are smaller groups of moms specifically designed to provide help and support when needed. It's easy for one mom to get lost in the shuffle of a large organization with many members. In a smaller care group, your members will have a chance to get to know each other better and to form friendships.

Too Much Work

Sometimes moms can become bogged down in the details of the playgroup, and will take on more than they can handle. If you find the playgroup becoming too much work, consider what you're doing. Playgroups are supposed to be fun and relaxing. If your group provides extra services that require extra work for you, consider if these services are necessary. If not, eliminate them. If they are necessary or desirable, delegate their management to someone else in the group. Surely there is another mom in the group who would like to get more involved. The bottom line is that you don't have to do everything. Share the load.

Membership Dues

Small neighborhood playgroups generally do not charge membership dues. The leaders usually absorb the expenses of printing copies of a phone list and a calendar because the costs are so minimal. However, if your group offers very many extra services and benefits that cost money to provide, such as a newsletter, you should consider charging membership dues or organizing fundraisers. Determine the expenses before you set the dues.

To avoid the perception that the playgroup has become a business, remind your members that the dues are donations that reimburse your out-of-pocket expenses only. Your time is still volunteered.

Losing the Leader

While playgroup members may fluctuate because of families moving, children starting school, or moms going back to work, these situations may very well involve the leader of the playgroup occasionally. When this happens, the group has a few options. Simply pass the baton to a new leader who feels as strongly about the playgroup as you do. Alternatively, the group can vote on a new leader. The playgroup doesn't have to end just because the leader no longer participates.

CHAPTER 12

CREATING SPECIALTY PLAYGROUPS

Playgroups are not exclusive to toddlers or preschoolers. Anyone can form a playgroup and benefit from the playgroup experience. You can start a playgroup exclusively for homeschoolers, or for boys only or girls only. There are playgroups for adopted children, premature babies, children with English as their second language, and children with special needs, whether physical, mental, emotional, or learning disabilities. You may have an only child and want to meet others with one child. You may want to design a playgroup for first-time parents, single parents, younger moms, older moms, working moms, and even at-home dads. Playgroups may form for families with specific ethnic or religious backgrounds. Any specialty playgroup can benefit from the suggestions and tips in this book with just a tweak here and there.

Homeschoolers

As the number of homeschooling families in our nation rises steadily each year, organizations and support groups are springing up to assist these families. Most homeschool playgroups derive from these support groups, where the parents conduct business while the children play. If you are trying to start a homeschool playgroup, go through your homeschool directory if you have one and mark those families in your area or those families which have children your children's ages. Call them or send them a letter explaining your intention to start a homeschool play-group. Also, post flyers at churches, libraries, bookstores, parks and community centers.

Homeschool playgroups present a unique situation because members may vary in age from infant to young teen. Nevertheless, the children still need supervision, preferably by adults. Supervision may be assigned, rotated among the membership or provided by a paid caretaker.

If the homeschool group is large enough, separate playgroups may be formed among boys or girls of particular ages or interests. However, because of the nature of homeschooling, older and younger siblings of various ages may have to be included during the playgroup time.

Although many detractors of homeschooling question the apparent lack of socialization of homeschooled children, the contrary is generally true. Homeschooled children spend time with and learn to feel com-fortable around both older and younger kids, rather than spend time with only their peer group. Homeschool playgroups are an excellent environment in which to do this.

However, if the group plans any particular activities, such as crafts or games for the children, you need to keep in mind this wide range of ages and abilities. What may interest one group will be too babyish for another, or too difficult as the case may be. Simply divide everyone into smaller groups and provide a variety of activities, such as board games, simple and elaborate crafts. Perhaps request that members bring some games from home. That should present you with an assortment of games for preschoolers to teens. You could also sing songs and organize relay races, foot races and simple ball games like dodge ball. They can all be altered to suit a particular range of ages or abilities.

Because of the size of homeschool playgroups, hosting the group in members' homes may be too risky of a venture to attempt. Instead, try to find a central location, such as a church or community center. A facility with a playground would be ideal. A park may work; however, a public park may be crowded with other groups, even during school hours.

Most homeschool groups tend to prefer school hours in which to meet. Early afternoon is generally preferred, giving the families time in the morning to finish their schoolwork for the day. Early afternoon is also an ideal time in which to go on field trips. Again, this is a time in which other children are in school.

Field trips provide excellent opportunities for homeschool playgroups to do something different and to learn at the same time. Check out the yellow pages of the phone book to find businesses your group may like to visit besides the usual museums, fire stations and libraries. Many businesses open their doors to groups for "behind the scenes" field trips if they are only asked, and this includes grocery stores, fast food restaurants, bakeries, dry cleaners, television stations, radio stations, airports, repair shops.

Little Boys Only or Little Girls Only

Little Zachary enjoys going to Mom's Day Out at church, but all the children his age are girls. Or the neighborhood is full of children, but the only little girl who was Ashley's age has just moved. These scenarios are repeated, with little variation, in cities across the nation. The solution? Start a playgroup specifically for boy toddlers or only for preschool girls.

The best way to find little boys or little girls in need of playgroups is by word of mouth. When I wanted to start the "Little Buddies" playgroup for preschool boys, I asked everyone in the Millbrook Area Playgroup if they knew any other moms with little boys. Only one mom did. From her lead, the special playgroup was up and running with five members within a month because that first mom knew of another mom of little boys who was interested, and she knew another mom who was interested, etc. So follow up on any information you get about "friends of friends" searching for little friends for their daughter or son. Get the word out at regular playgroups or mothers' groups by contacting the leaders or by posting flyers where these groups meet. Also, don't forget to post flyers at pediatricians' offices as well as parks and libraries.

Playgroups of this sort are generally kept small and intimate so that the little participants can get to know each other and so their parents can supervise their activities more easily. Small groups facilitate more structured activities and provide an opportunity for moms to join in the activities as well.

Activities for these playgroups can be tailored to suit the ages, interests and abilities of the children. You aren't limited to free play only. However, you need to decide if older and younger siblings are invited. If so, they may find the structured activities unsuited to their tastes. Their mothers should be prepared to bring special toys or activities to keep them occupied.

Adopted Children

Parents may actually find playgroups designed for adopted children more beneficial than the children themselves will. Many so-called "regular" playgroups include adopted children from time to time. However, adoptive parents share unique concerns above and beyond the usual parenting problems, and they may feel a need to share these concerns with other parents in the same situation who can understand and empathize. Having support from others who have "been there" means a great deal.

Seek adoptive parents by posting flyers around the community or contacting local agencies. Word of mouth is another means of finding others interested in joining a playgroup for adopted children. On the Internet, visit www.adoptnet.org, a web site for adoptive parents by the National Adoption Center.

Premature Babies

Playgroups for premature babies are prevalent in cities with neonatal units. Some hospitals offer support groups to the parents, and playgroups often form from these. To find other moms interested in starting a playgroup, contact the local hospitals and pediatricians in the area. See if they will let you post flyers. Also, search the Internet for national organizations. Their web sites should list local chapters from which you can organize a playgroup.

These playgroups tend to be small, which gives the moms an opportunity to foster friendships, share experiences, and find advice and empathy. The playgroup could function as free playtime for the children or you could organize activities suitable to their abilities. Again, older siblings may need to bring their own items to play with during playgroup.

Children with Special Needs

Playgroups designed for children with special needs may double as a support group for their parents. Many times, playgroups form out of support groups of parents of special needs children. Surf the Internet for nationally organized support groups by searching for a particular disability in the search engines. From their web sites, you may find a local chapter or support group near you with playgroups offered as a benefit to its members. If not, get the information you need to start a chapter. If none of these are available, use your doctors or therapists as sources for finding other children who may benefit from the specialized playgroup and place an ad in the newspaper as well.

The age ranges may vary too much to organize activities. But once the group has gathered, all of the members can decide if they will have activities geared to the children's abilities or simply provide free playtime. This type of playgroup gives the children involved a chance to be with others facing the same challenges. Feeling part of a peer group fosters self-esteem.

Some playgroups for children with special needs are able to get a professional therapist to join the group. Sometimes state agencies will provide a therapist free of charge, but if you can't find one, perhaps a therapist will lead the group activities during part of the playgroup session for a nominal fee. Ask around. Even if you can't find a therapist to join you, the parents can organize and lead the group in appropriate structured activities or let the children just enjoy free playtime together.

Younger and Older Moms

Just as the ages of children in a playgroup may vary, so will the ages of the parents involved. However, teenage moms who are much younger than the other mothers in a playgroup may feel uncomfortable. At the same time, women who waited later in life to start their family may feel out of place because they are much older than the other moms in the playgroup. Nevertheless, parenting concerns are basically the same the world over; everyone deals with colic, potty training, and sibling rivalry. However, younger and older moms may feel more comfortable in playgroups where they are the norm rather than the exception and where they have more in common with the other members than just their children.

Finding other moms who are interested in joining the playgroup will be your biggest obstacle, just as it is for any playgroup. Use the same methods suggested for typical playgroups. Place ads in newspapers, post flyers around the community, surf the Internet, and ask around. In addition, teen moms may seek like-minded moms from parenting classes at the local hospital or community center. Older moms may ask their fertility specialists for the names of other parents who may be interested in starting a playgroup or for the chance to post flyers in their offices.

Don't forget the Internet as a possible avenue for finding others who may be interested. The web sites with playgroup directories, such as OnlinePlaygroup.com, have many special playgroups for younger or older moms. Also, check out online parenting magazines.

Because your group may be composed of both at-home and working parents, prepare to be flexible regarding scheduling issues. You may not be able to meet as frequently as you would like, or you may have to choose a day that's not quite as convenient as anther day would be for you. Nevertheless, this playgroup will offer you and your child an opportunity to meet and make friends with others in similar situations, so take advantage of it! Get to know the other parents, and meet for playdates between playgroup sessions at times that are more convenient.

Working Moms and Single Parents

Just like stay-at-home moms, working moms and single parents want to spend time with their children and develop friendships that include their children. The best ways to find them are to place ads in the newspaper, post flyers around the community, and ask around. Get your friends and co-workers to ask around as well. You would be surprised how quickly a playgroup can form from just word-of-mouth advertising!

With working and single parents, you must be flexible regarding days, times and frequency of playgroup. Saturday may be the only convenient day for everyone, so a biweekly playgroup may work best. This would allow some Saturdays to be spent in family activities. Even so, many of them may not be able to participate in every playgroup meeting, but don't let that prevent you and one or two others from getting together regularly.

At-Home Dads

We can't forget those at-home dads! More and more dads are staying home as the primary caregiver of their children every year. They need the acceptance and understanding a playgroup can provide just as much as a stay-at-home mom does. Although most playgroups welcome at-home dads and their children, being the only male in the group may make you somewhat uncomfortable at first. Don't let that discourage you from participating, if only for your children's sakes. Besides, you can use this opportunity to observe how a playgroup is organized before starting your own group for at-home dads.

Some national groups are designed specifically for at-home dads. Dad-to-Dad is an organization connecting at-home dads with others in their area. Visit the web site at www.slowlane.com and consider starting a local chapter. Slowlane.com also features other valuable resources for its members.

A playgroup for dads and their children doesn't necessarily mean at-home dads only. If the group meets on the weekend or in the evening, working fathers may be able to participate. The children can enjoy free playtime while the dads talk about their interests, watch a game or play cards. The group can meet at a local park or attend a sporting event.

Also, the group can organize activities such as building a birdhouse, hiking through the woods, camping overnight, or playing T-ball.

Just like a general membership playgroup, getting the word out is one of the most difficult aspects of starting an at-home dad playgroup. In addition to placing ads in the newspaper and posting flyers around the community, ask local mothers' groups if they have received requests from other at-home dads. Also, seek out dads from other groups with similar interests, like other football fans or computer technicians, for example. Broach the subject of getting together sometime with your children and invite those who seem interested to meet at a local park. If all goes well, suggest that the group continues on a regular basis. Chances are that one or two of the other dads will know someone else who may like to participate.

Ethnic and Religious

Cities with a large percentage of multicultural residents often have playgroups geared toward specific ethnic or religious backgrounds. However, even in small towns, if certain ethnic or religious communities are large enough, the parents will form playgroups so their children will have friends of a similar background. Really, such is the case with all specialty playgroups; after all, homeschoolers want to know other homeschoolers, at-home dads want to spend time with other at-home dads, and parents of children with special needs want to get to know other parents and their children.

Seek other parents who may want to join your group through your community, by placing ads in the newspapers, posting flyers, and asking around. Churches, synagogues and mosques are excellent locations for flyers. On the Internet, search for your particular ethnic background or religion. You may be surprised to find an organization near you that offers playgroups as a benefit for its members.

Because your group may be composed of both at-home and working parents, prepare to be flexible regarding scheduling issues. You may not be able to meet as frequently as you would like, or you may have to choose a day that's not quite as convenient as anther day would be for you. Nevertheless, this playgroup will offer you and your child an opportunity to meet and make friends, so take advantage of it! Get to know the other parents, and meet for playdates at times that are more convenient in addition to the regular playgroup sessions.

CHAPTER 13

NATIONAL ORGANIZATIONS

You may feel isolated and lonely right now, but you are not alone and you won't be lonely for very much longer! Very quickly you will find other stay-at-home moms yearning for the same companionship you are. Some have already made the step you are about to make and have founded playgroups and mothers' organizations, some of which have expanded on a national scale.

As a matter of fact, there may be a local chapter in your hometown, and you may feel more comfortable joining an existing local chapter. All the initial legwork will have already been done for you, and all the extra services in place. Or you may be interested in starting a local chapter if there isn't already one near you. Many of these national organizations provide start-up kits and assist in various ways with helping to form new chapters. Although they do charge annual dues, the dues are minimal and they cover a variety of services.

Keep in mind, however, the kind of playgroup you and your child want. Although national organizations boast thousands of satisfied members, they may not offer the kind of group you are searching for. One of the best reasons for starting your own playgroup is to make it exactly the way you want it to be. You may not want to get bogged down in keeping up with dues, publishing a newsletter, arranging for accommodations, or scheduling special speakers. Your personal budget may not allow the extra expense of membership dues, or you may not want to be separated from your child, especially if he already attends a pre-school program a few days a week.

But, if being involved in both a national mothers' group and a play-group interests you, maybe you should consider joining both. Many organizations offer organized playgroups as a benefit for its members. If the one in your area does not have this service, you may meet other moms there who would want to join you in starting a playgroup.

Check out their web sites and see what you think.

Dad-To-Dad

Started in January 1995, Dad-to-Dad brings at-home dads together to share information and receive positive reinforcement through chil-dren's playgroups, dads' night out dinners and newsletters.

Address: At-Home Dad, 61 Brightwood Ave, North Andover, MA 01845
Web site: http://www.slowlane.com/d2d

MOMS Clubs International

MOMS Clubs, which stand for Moms Offering Moms Support, can be found nationwide. This web site is their official international site and it has information and links to many other local MOMS Clubs.

Address: New Groups, MOMS Club, c/o 25371 Rye Canyon, Valencia, CA 91355
Web site: http://www.momsclub.org
Email: momsclub@aol.com

MOPS—Mothers Of Pre-Schoolers

MOPS is a non-denominational Christian organization open to all mothers with children under school age.

Address: MOPS International, Inc., P.O. Box 102200, Denver, CO 80250–2200

Phone: (303) 733–5353
Web site: http://www.gospelcom.net/mops
Email: info@mops.org

Mothers and More

Mothers and More, which used to be F.E.M.A.L.E. (Formerly Employed Mothers At the Leading Edge), is an international not-for-profit organization supporting sequencing mothers—women who have altered their career paths in order to care for their children at home.

Address: Mothers and More National Office, P.O. Box 31, Elmhurst, IL 60126
Phone: (630) 941-3553
Web site: http://www.mothersandmore.org
Email: nationaloffice@mothersandmore.org

National Association of Mothers' Centers

The National Association of Mothers' Centers was created to offer support to new mothers and families and help them find answers to their questions. It is a national, "grassroots" organization made up of mothers nationwide.

Address: National Association of Mothers' Centers, 64 Division Avenue, Levittown, NY 11756
Phone: (800) 645–3828 or (516) 520–2929
Web site: http://www.yourbaby.com/consumer/resources/namc.asp
Email: info@motherscenter.org

National Online Fathers of Twins Club

With current members from all parts of the United States, Canada, Great Britain, and more, the NOFOTC's database contains enough names to be able to put fathers together with other fathers in their own area. As an organization for fathers of multiples, the goal is to be a support line and resource for information on parenting, and specifically fathering, of multiples.

Address: NOFOTC c/o Jeff Maxwell, 2804 NW 163rd, Edmond, OK 73012

Web site: http://www.nofotc.org

Email: membership@nototc.org

National Organization of Mothers of Twins Clubs, Inc.

This organization is a network of some 475 local clubs representing over 21,000 individual parents of multiples—twins, triplets and quadruplets.

Address: NOMOTC Executive Office, P.O. Box 438, Thompson Station, TN 37179–0438

Phone: (615) 595–0936 or 1–877–540–2200

Web site: http://www.nomotc.org

Email: nomotc@aol.com

CHAPTER 14

ADDITIONAL RESOURCES

Here are some additional resources for playgroups and at-home parents that you may find helpful.

Internet Resources for Playgroup Directories

OnlinePlaygroup.com
PlaydateConnection.com
Slowlane.com

Internet Resources for Crafts for Adults

CraftCentralStation.com
CraftsFairOnline.com
CraftsInc.com

Internet Resources for Activities for Children

FamilyFun.com
ParentSoup.com
TheIdeaBox.com

Books for At-Home Moms

Gochnauer, Cheryl. *So You Want to Be a Stay-at-Home Mom.* InterVarsity Press, 1999.

Otto, Donna and Elisabeth Elliot. *The Stay-at-Home Mom.* Harvest House Publ. Inc., 1997.

Peters, Angie. *Celebrate Home: Great Ideas for Stay-at-Home Moms.* Concordia Publishing House, 1998.

Tinglov, Christina Baglivi. *The Stay-at-Home Parent Survival Guide: Real-Life Advice from Moms, Dads, and Other Experts A to Z.* NTC Publishing Group, 2000.

Books for At-home Dads

Oberle, Joseph. *Diary of a Mad Househusband: Musing on Life as a Stay-at-Home Dad.* Kimm Publishing, Inc., 1996.

Singletary, Mike and Russ Pate. *Daddy's Home at Last: What it Takes for Dads to Put Families First.* Zondervan Publishing House, 1998.

Tinglov, Christina Baglivi. *The Stay-at-Home Parent Survival Guide: Real-Life Advice from Moms, Dads, and Other Experts A to Z.* NTC Publishing Group, 2000.

Books on Activities for Children

Broad, Laura Peabody and Nancy Towner Butterworth. *The Playgroup Handbook.* St. Martin's Press, 1974.

Munger, Evelyn Moats and Susan J. Bowden. *Beyond Peek-a-Boo and Pat-A-Cake: Activities for Baby's First 24 Months.* New Win Publishing Inc., 1993.

Press, Judy and Loretta Trezzo Braren. *Big Fun Craft Book: Creative Fun for 2 to 6-Year-Olds.* Williamson Publishing Company, 1995.

Silberg, Jackie and Linda Greigg. *Games to Play with Babies.* Gryphon House, Inc., 1995.

About the Author

Carren W. Joye, a homeschooling mom of four children, has founded five successful playgroups and has assisted countless playgroups worldwide via the Internet. Joye, who holds the B.A. from Coker College in S.C., currently lives in Alabama with her family and maintains the playgroup and homeschool web sites.

Appendix

Appendix A

Use this flyer to attract new members to an existing group. Post copies in your community and distribute copies in various neighborhoods.

Millbrook Area Playgroup

Thursdays, 9:30 a.m. to 11:30 a.m.

In an effort to get to know our neighbors, a few stay-at-home moms have formed a playgroup in the Millbrook area for our infants, toddlers, and preschool children. It is a wonderful opportunity for our children to play together and for the adults to socialize.

Playgroup gives us a chance to make new friends, especially for those who are new to the area, feel isolated in neighborhoods without children, do not have relatives nearby or are first-time parents. We are primarily, but not exclusively, stay-at-home moms who realize a need for social interaction for our children.

We generally meet every Thursday from 9:30 a.m. to 11:30 a.m. Because it is a rotating playgroup, the locations vary depending on who hosts it each week. Playgroup is free; all we ask is your participation! If you would like more information, please give us a call. We hope to hear from you!

Your Name
Your phone number

Another Mom's Name (if possible)
Her phone number

Put your web site address here!

Appendix B

Flyers like this one can be distributed in area neighborhoods to start your playgroup. Use it as a flyer or reformat it as a letter.

Neighborhood Playgroup

Like many of you, I am a stay-at-home mom with young children. In an effort to get to know some of you, I would like to start a playgroup in our area for our infants, toddlers and preschool children. It would be a wonderful opportunity for our children to play together and for the adults to socialize. Playgroup would give us and our children a chance to make new friends, especially for those of us who are new to the area, do not have relatives nearby or are first-time parents.

Playgroup is free; all we need is your participation! If you are interested in forming this weekly playgroup, please call me by (Day and Date) to let me know what days and times are convenient for you. I look forward to hearing from you!

Your Name
Your phone number

Index

Conflicts
       Among Children, 12, 41, 54, 111, 118, 119, 121, 125
       Among Adults, 66, 111, 124-125
Cost, 4–5, 13, 18–20, 69–70, 72, 75–76, 81, 128, 135
Couples' Night Out, 68
Crafts, see also Activities, Games, Songs
       For adults, 34, 70, 151
       For Children, 0–1, 8, 12, 19, 24, 26, 34–35, 56, 76, 92, 122, 134,
       142, 151–152
              Binoculars, Paper Roll, 90
              Christmas Tree, 104
              Collage, Leaf, 101
              Collage, Picture, 101
              Cookies, 82, 102
              Drawing, Lifesize, 103
              Drawing Pictures, 82, 88
              Drum, 90
              Easter Basket, 92
              Finger paint, 82, 100
              Hand prints, with Paint, 96
              Hand prints, with Plaster, 99
              Masks, Paper Plate, 91
              Mobile, Shapes, 92
              New Year's Day Crown, 87
              Paper Bag Puppets, 87
              Play-doh, 82, 99
              Reindeer Hands and Feet, 105
              Santa Claus Face, 105
              Sparklers, 97
              Sun Catchers, 91
              Tambourine, 89
              T-shirt, 47, 95

Activities for, 8, 15, 17, 34, 51, 76, 78, 81, 134, 140, 151–152
Articles on, 34, 26-28
Definition of, xix
Existing, 23–25, 33, 147, 157
Guidelines for, see Guidelines
Hosting, 13–14, 40, 42–43, 51, 53, 56, 75–76, 115, 128, 138
Length of
Promotion of, 25-31, 32, 129
Size of, 5, 8, 13, 15, 22, 52, 63, 91, 108, 122, 138
Time it takes to get one started, 20-21, 29, 122-123
Types of, 4-5, 58, 137
Web site for, 20, 33–35, 76, 141
Playtime, 0–1, 7–8, 15, 22, 55, 80–81, 87, 118–119, 141–142, 144
Postcards, 19–20, 30, 33
Posters, 19, 25, 74, 129
Premature Babies, 4, 137, 141
Press Releases, 26, 112
Project Night, 67
Problems, 35, 45, 61, 111, 118, 121–125, 131, 141
Purpose, 6, 12, 38

Recipe Exchange, 63, 70
Recruiting, 20, 27, 112, 129
Resources for A-Home Parents, 151-153
Rotation, 17–18, 40–41, 53, 114, 128, 132
Rules, see also Guidelines

Samples
Flyers, 6, 18–21, 25, 29–30, 32–33, 74, 112, 129–130, 138, 140–141, 143, 145–146, 159
Postcards, 19–20, 30, 33
Posters, 19, 25, 74, 129

Printed in the United States
4121